Panzer Crewman

1939–45

Gordon Williamson • Illustrated by Velimir Vuksic

First published in Great Britain in 2002 by Osprey Publishing, Elms Court, Chapel Way, Botley, Oxford OX2 9LP, United Kingdom.
Email: info@ospreypublishing.com

ISBN 1 84176 328 4

Editor: Thomas Lowres
Design: Ken Vail Graphic Design, Cambridge, UK
Index by Alan Thatcher
Originated by Magnet Harlequin, Uxbridge, UK
Printed in China through World Print Ltd.

02 03 04 05 06   10 9 8 7 6 5 4 3 2 1

For a catalogue of all books published by Osprey Military and Aviation please contact:

The Marketing Manager, Osprey Direct UK, PO Box 140, Wellingborough, Northants, NN8 4ZA, United Kingdom.
Email: info@ospreydirect.co.uk

The Marketing Manager, Osprey Direct USA, c/o Motorbooks International, PO Box 1, Osceola, WI 54020-0001, USA.
Email: info@ospreydirectusa.com

www.ospreypublishing.com

Artist's note

Readers may care to note that the original paintings from which the colour plates in this book were prepared are available for private sale. All reproduction copyright whatsoever is retained by the Publishers. All enquiries should be addressed to:

Velimir Vuksic,
Ilica 54,
10000 Zagreb,
Croatia

The Publishers regret that they can enter into no correspondence upon this matter.

Acknowledgements

I would like to thank all those who provided the many excellent photographs used in this work. The images are credited individually, but I would like to single out for special thanks, Herr Robert Noss of Germany for the use of so many excellent photographs. A large part of Herr Noss' superb photographic collection is available to view on his fine website, details of which are provided in the Museums and Collections section of this book.

FRONT COVER **A Panzer hauptmann in the cupola of his Panzer IV. (Robert Noss)**

CONTENTS

PANZER CREWMAN 1939–45

INTRODUCTION

The British Army was the first military force to make successful use of what was to become universally known as 'the tank'. The effect of the 28-ton Mk I vehicles sent into action at Flers in September 1916, however, was more psychological than actual, as many became bogged down in mud or in craters, and the attack drew scorn from the many detractors of the new weapon. The attack on the German positions at Cambrai in November 1917 was far more successful, with tanks for the first time used as a breakthrough weapon in their own right rather than merely providing infantry support. The degree of success was greater than had been anticipated, but mechanical breakdown, combat losses and the lack of sufficient reserves to exploit the progress made by the tanks, prevented even greater glory.

The Germans were startled by the early achievements of Britain's tanks and began rapid development of their own. The result was the 32-ton A7V, which was armed with a 5.7-cm gun and manned by a crew of 18. A7Vs, along with a number of captured British tanks, were sent into action at Villers-Bretonneux in April 1918. It was the world's first tank-versus-tank engagement, but poor mechanical reliability and lack of sufficient trench-crossing capability once again mitigated against any significant achievements.

The rapidly deteriorating military situation saw the war end before German tank development could provide its armies with a truly effective battle tank.

Germany's post-war military strength was greatly diminished, with the new Reichswehr restricted to a size of just 100,000, but while manpower had been reduced, events at Cambrai had revealed the true potential of the tank for the future. Hauptmann Heinz Guderian was particularly keen to ensure that the vanquished Germans focused their military redevelopment around the tank, albeit in a new role. Guderian could see that the concept of the tank as a heavy, slow-moving, fire platform, advancing at only the pace of the infantry it supported would never see its full potential realised.

Through the 1920s Guderian studied tank tactics, and in 1931 he was appointed to command 3. Kraftfahrabteilung in Berlin. It was whilst in command of this unit that Guderian devised the idea of dressing up ordinary vehicles with mock tank superstructures and turrets made from cardboard and plywood in order to carry out basic tank training exercises. Guderian's big break came after the

Generaloberst Heinz Guderian, born in 1888 of a West Prussian military family, is generally accepted as being the father of the German armoured forces. He was decorated with the Knight's Cross on 27 October 1939 for his command of XIX Army Corps during the attack on Poland, and to this was added the Oakleaves on 10 July 1941 for his leadership of 2nd Panzergruppe during the invasion of the Soviet Union. As with many of Germany's best soldiers, he fell from favour with Hitler, and was dismissed from his post as Inspector General of Panzertruppe. He died in 1954.

accession to power of Adolf Hitler and the National Socialists. Hitler took a keen interest in tank warfare, and after seeing a demonstration at the Kummersdorf training grounds in October 1934 he became an avid supporter of the foundation of a tank corps for the German Army. With Hitler as an ally Guderian's star was firmly in the ascendant, despite the dissenting voices of traditionalists within the German Army.

Guderian's book, *Achtung Panzer!*, was published in 1938 and put forward his views on tank tactics. He advocated the use of the tank independent of the infantry, proceeding at its own best pace and with the sheer power of massed pincer-formation tank attacks, encircling and crushing the enemy. By 1939 Guderian had risen to the rank of general, and in October of that year he was appointed Inspekteur der Panzertruppe.

With a new war on the horizon, the world was about to discover just how much the German military had learned from the painful experiences of the First World War.

CHRONOLOGY

15 September 1916	First ever tank action at Flers on the Somme.
24 April 1918	First ever tank-versus-tank action, at Villers Bretonneux.
July 1934	Production of the 5.4-ton Panzerkampfwagen I begins.
Spring 1935	The first of the 7.6-ton Panzerkampfwagen IIs appear.
15 October 1935	1. Panzer Division is formed in Weimar under Generalleutnant Baron Maximilian von Weichs.
1936	The Panzerkampfwagen III, at 15 tons, and the Panzer IV, at 17.3 tons, go into production.
7 October 1936	German tanks arrive in Spain to support Franco's Nationalist troops during the civil war.
1 September 1939	War erupts. The Blitzkrieg begins. Over 3,000 Panzers go into action in the three-pronged attack on Poland, but around 1,000 are lost.
10 May 1940	The campaign in the west begins. Some 2,400 Panzers go into action, but of that total around 1,400 are Mk Is armed with only machine guns. They will face over 3,000 Allied tanks.
14 February 1941	The first units of what will become Rommel's 'Panzerarmee Afrika' arrive in Tripoli.
22 June 1941	Operation Barbarossa, the invasion of the Soviet Union, begins. Around 3,750 Panzers roll into Russia, divided into four Panzergruppen.
1 December 1941	Army Group Centre's armoured assault on Moscow comes to a halt just short of the city's suburbs.
29 January 1942	Rommel captures Benghazi.
20 June 1942	Rommel captures Tobruk.
23 October 1942	Rommel's exhausted Panzers, which failed to capture El Alamein, are smashed by a massive British counter-attack.
August 1942	First of the 55-ton Panzerkampfwagen VI 'Tiger' tanks roll off the production line. The tanks see action for the first time, on the Leningrad front.
September 1942	First prototype 43-ton Panzerkampfwagen V 'Panther' produced.
16 February 1943	Soviets recapture Kharkov.
15 March 1943	II SS-Panzer Korps retake Kharkov.
5 July 1943	German offensive at Kursk, Operation Citadel, is launched and the greatest armoured battle of all time begins.
11-12 July 1943	In the battle of Prokhorovka, over 700 Soviet and German tanks are destroyed in just two days of fighting.
13 July 1943	Operation Citadel is called off.

November 1943	The mighty 69-ton Panzerkampfwagen VI 'Königstiger' goes into production.
23 December 1943	First trial runs of the ultimate heavy tank, the 188-ton Panzerkampfwagen 'Maus'.
6 June 1944	Allies land in Normandy opposed by nine Panzer divisions.
13 June 1944	A single Tiger tank commanded by SS-Hauptsturmführer Michael Witmann decimates the spearhead of British 22nd Armoured Brigade at Villers Bocage.
26 July 1944	A single Panther tank commanded by SS-Oberscharführer Ernst Barkmann halts an American advance on the road towards St. Lo. Barkmann personally knocks out 15 US tanks in just two days.
20 August 1944	Remaining German Panzer units in Normandy decimated during attempts to escape through the 'Falaise Gap'.
16–26 September 1944	Allied airborne landings at Arnhem defeated, principally by elements of 9. and 10. SS-Panzer Divisions.
16 December 1944	The last great German Panzer assault of the war starts as 6. Panzer Army launches its attack through the Ardennes, and the Battle of the Bulge begins.
26 December 1944	The German offensive finally runs out of steam, and on 8 January Hitler calls off the operation. The Panzertruppe will spend the last few months of the war in desperate and ultimately futile defensive actions on both Eastern and Western Fronts.

RECRUITMENT

Following the end of the First World War, the army of the new German Weimar Republic, the *Reichswehr*, was limited by the terms of the Treaty of Versailles to a mere 100,000 men, formed into seven infantry and three cavalry divisions. On the accession to power of the National

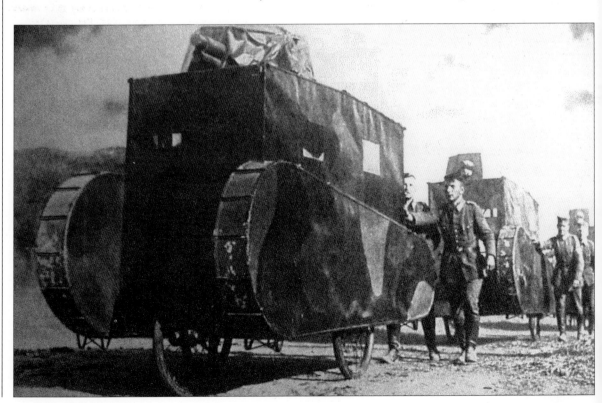

Examples of Germany's famous cardboard tanks on a training exercise in the late 1920s. These simple plywood and card superstructures were built over a standard automobile or, as in this case, a pedal-powered tricycle! They may have looked amusing, but the lessons learned on the training grounds helped Germany become one of the leading proponents of armoured warfare.

The *Soldbuch* of a Panzer soldier. Note the black Panzer jacket with its death's-head collar patches in the identity photograph. Note also that the initial rank of schütze is prefixed 'Panzer' to become 'Panzerschützen'.

Socialists, a rapid build-up of the armed forces began. Coupled with this, there was an explosion in the number of non-military organisations that provided covert military training. Each year, up to 300,000 Germans underwent a period of compulsory state labour in the *Reichs Arbeits Dienst* (RAD). Although much of the work carried out by the RAD involved construction or agriculture, it was a uniformed organisation, run on military lines and which carried out military style drill training (albeit carrying shovels rather than rifles).

In addition, political organisations also began to give discreet military training. For example, the party's flying corps, the *National Sozialistische Flieger Korps* (NSFK), was used to give basic flying training, and the motor corps, *National Sozialistische Kraftfahrkorps* (NSKK), gave driver training and instruction on vehicle maintenance.

The need for such subterfuge ended in 1935 when universal military conscription was reintroduced. All German males between the ages of 17 and 25 were required to register for military service. Up to the start of the Second World War it was possible to obtain a deferment of military service if the individual was undergoing some technical training, such as an apprenticeship. Ultimately however, the day would come when the prospective soldier was required to report for registration at his local *Wehrkreis* (Military District) offices. Here, his details would be registered, a medical examination undertaken, and any individual skills appropriate to a particular branch of the service were recorded. He would be allocated to the *Ersatz und Ausbildungs Abtleilung* (Replacement and Training Detachment) of his assigned unit, then allocated a *Wehrpass* (military ID book). This book would list the recruit's personal details, any special skills and languages, service in the RAD, and his intended unit. The *Wehrpass* was a personal ID, and it could also be used to prove that an individual had fulfilled his duty to register for military service.

Once the registration process was complete, the future soldier would return to his everyday civilian life and await the call-up papers that would eventually be sent to him by registered mail, instructing him when and where to report for duty.

Up until the point of registration, as with most armies, there was an element of choice available to the prospective soldier with regard to the particular branch he wished to serve in. However, once registered, the Wehrmacht was as likely as any other army to make totally illogical and perverse decisions in assigning soldiers to units that seemed totally inappropriate. So, needless to say, many young men volunteered before they were drafted, in order to have the chance of joining the military arm of their choice.

Prior to the introduction of conscription in 1935 it was normal for prospective soldiers to volunteer for their own choice of Waffengattung (Branch of Service) in the normal way. However, given that the first Panzer regiments were only formed in 1934, not long before the introduction of compulsory military service, it is safe to assume that the vast majority of Panzer soldiers were registered after the introduction of conscription. German soldiers on active service in the Second World

Three typical examples of German recruiting posters for the Panzerwaffe, with exhortations such as 'Panzer – Your Weapon!', 'Volunteers Forward!' and 'Come Join Us!'.

War fell into two basic categories, the *Berufsoldat* (career soldier), and those considered *Auf Kriegsdauer* (in for the duration), who would eventually return to civilian life. The Panzertruppe would have been no different to any other branch in containing a mixture of both.

In common with many other armies, the Wehrmacht's initial group of armoured soldiers were drawn from cavalry regiments that had been mechanised to become Panzer regiments. As a result, many of those who found themselves serving in tanks would originally have been recruited as cavalrymen.

After the outbreak of war, the Panzer featured regularly and prominently in both newspaper and newsreel reports of Germany's initial stunning successes during the Blitzkrieg period. The National Socialists made extremely effective use of propaganda, and were aware that dramatic photographs could make an instant impact. As a result, they ensured that the German newspapers and magazines of the time had a high photographic content. Magazines such as the famed *Signal*, which was translated into many languages, including English, were years ahead of their time in the use of colour photography. Even by today's standards, *Signal* was a well-designed magazine. Cleverly taken photos, usually from a low angle, were used to give the tank an even more impressive sense of mass, power and invincibility. Showing the proud commander in his turret cupola, dressed in smart black Panzer clothing, ensured that the *Panzerwaffe* maintained a very high profile in the eyes of the German populace. Unsurprisingly, there was no shortage of recruits for this elite branch of the Wehrmacht.

The *SS-Verfügungstruppe*

At this juncture, it is worth also mentioning recruitment into the *SS-Verfügungstruppe* (SS-VT), the forerunner of the Waffen-SS, which would eventually field some of the Second World War's most powerful armoured divisions. Enlistment into the SS-VT was entirely voluntary. The Wehrmacht jealously guarded its status as the nation's *Waffenträger* (sole bearer of arms) and did all it could to ensure that the expansionist aims of Reichsführer-SS Heinrich Himmler were held in check. One important concession granted was that service in the SS-VT was to be considered as having fulfilled the individual's obligation for compulsory military service, thus, in some ways at least, equating service in the SS-VT to service in the Wehrmacht.

At this point in time, prior to the outbreak of war, there existed no SS Panzer units *as such*, but it is worth noting that many of the war's top Panzer aces were from the Waffen-SS and had joined the SS-VT in these early days. Recruitment into the SS-VT was very selective, and it is interesting to note some of the qualifications for service in the military branch of the SS. The following information is taken from an original wartime recruiting leaflet entitled *Wie komme ich zur SS-Verfügungstruppe* (*How do I join the SS-VT?*).

SS-VT candidates had to:
(i)   be between the ages of 17 and 22.
(ii) be physically fit for service in the SS.
(iii) have an acceptable political outlook.
(iv) provide evidence of Aryan ancestry back to 1800.

The special version of the Panzer I used for tank driver training also had other uses. Here it is used as a fully tracked hearse as the Panzerwaffe says farewell to one of its own. (Wade Krawczyk)

(v) be neither married nor engaged to be married.

(vi) have fulfilled RAD obligation.

(vii) have parents' written permission if at the minimum entry age of 17.

(viii) if undergoing professional training such as an apprenticeship, to have completed the course or obtained a release from the appropriate supervisor.

(ix) pay for any dental treatment required to bring the applicant up to standard before enlistment.

(x) have good eyesight without glasses.

(xi) have no criminal record, or criminal proceedings pending.

Geographical recruitment

In general terms, recruitment into the Panzerwaffe was done on a geographical basis. Recruits who joined or were conscripted in a particular area were likely to end up in the local unit. However, this was not a universal policy, and in each local unit there would also be a scattering of individuals from other parts of the Reich. The principal demographic mix in each Panzer division would be roughly as shown in the following chart. The chart indicates the number or name of the unit, the date it was either founded or was converted into a Panzer division, its controlling Wehrkreis and home town where appropriate, and the area from which it drew most of its personnel, again if a specific region was predominant.

Panzer Division	Founded	Wehrkreis	Make-up
1	1935	IX (Weimar)	Saxons, Thuringians
2	1935	XVIII (Vienna)	Austrians
3	1935	III (Berlin)	Prussians
4	1938	XIII (Würzburg)	Bavarians
5	1938	VIII (Oppeln)	Silesians, Sudetenlanders
6	1939	VI (Wüppertal)	Westphalians

7	1939	IX (Gera)	Thüringians
8	1939	III (Cottbus)	Prussians
9	1939	XVII (Vienna)	Austrians
10	1939	V (Stuttgart)	various
11	1940	VIII (Görlitz)	Silesians
12	1940	II (Stettin)	Prussians
13	1940	XI (Magdeburg)	
14	1940	IV (Dresden)	formed from 4 and 14 Inf Divs
15	1941	XII (Kaiserslautern)	
16	1941	VI (Munster)	Westphalians
17	1940	VII (Augsburg)	Swabians
18	1940	IV	formed from 4 and 14 Inf Divs
19	1940	XI (Hanover)	
20	1940	IX (Gotha)	Hessians
21	1941	III (Berlin)	Prussians
22	1940	XII	
23	1940	V	formed in occupied France
24	1941	III (Frankfurt a.d.O.)	Prussians
25	1942	VI	formed in occupied Norway
26	1942	III (Berlin)	Prussians
27	1942		formed in occupied France
116	1943	VI (Rheine)	
130 (Panzer Lehr)	1944	III (Berlin)	formed from demonstration units from the Panzer Schools
155 Reserve	1943	V (Ulm)	various
179 Reserve	1943	IX (Weimar)	various
233 Reserve	1943	III (Frankfurt a d O.)	various
273 Reserve	1943	XIII	various
'Clausewitz'	1945		ad hoc unit raised from Hitler Youth boys
'Holstein'	1945	X	various
'Münchberg'	1945	IV	various
'Norwegen'	1943		raised in Oslo, occupied Norway
2 SS 'Das Reich'	1942		formed from the old SS-Verfügungsdivision
3 SS 'Totenkopf'	1942		Berlin-Oranienburg
5 SS 'Wiking'	1943		Hamburg & Klagenfurt
9 SS 'Hohenstaufen'	1943		formed in north-eastern occupied France
10 SS 'Frundsberg'	1943		formed in south-western occupied France
12 SS 'Hitlerjugend'	1944		formed in occupied Belgium

There are a small number of important Panzer units that deserve separate mention because they differed, in many ways, particularly in their recruitment procedures, from more conventional units that were organised around regional links.

Panzer Division *Grossdeutschland*

This extremely powerful and important unit had its origins in the elite Berlin Guard regiment. In 1936 the then commander-in-chief of the army, Generaloberst Werner von Fritsch, required each army unit to send the men best trained in drill movements to serve with the Guard, which performed numerous guard and ceremonial duties in the Reichshauptstadt, Berlin. The regiment wore a distinctive shoulder strap cipher, the Gothic letter 'W' (for 'Wache'). In June 1939, von Fritsch's successor Generaloberst Walter von Brauchitsch renamed the Guard Regiment *Infanterieregiment 'Grossdeutschland'*, bestowing on the unit its own cuff band and shoulder strap cipher 'GD'. Continuing the policy of recruiting only the finest men, *Grossdeutschland* signed up men from every corner of the Reich. The unit grew to divisional size (and ultimately into a Panzerkorps) and was designated a Panzer division in 1943.

Panzer Division *Feldherrnhalle*

Based in Danzig, this unit's associations were political rather than regional. The division was closely linked to the elite *Feldherrnhalle* Standarte of the SA stormtroopers and indeed wore the same cuff band, on SA brown material. The unit shoulder cipher was the so-called SA Kampfrune, and even the unit banner was the Party's Deutschland Erwache style swastika banner, rather than the traditional army standard bearing the Iron Cross and Wehrmacht eagle. The unit was expanded from regimental size, achieving divisional status as 60 Panzer Grenadier Division *Feldherrnhalle* in 1944. Within the division, the armoured element was 160 Panzer Battalion *'Feldherrnhalle'*. A second division, this time of Panzer division status, was raised in 1945 with cadres from 60 Panzer Grenadier Division and known as Panzer Division *Feldherrnhalle* (2). The two divisions formed Panzerkorps *Feldherrnhalle*.

Fallschirmpanzer Division *Hermann Göring*

The origins of this massive formation lay with an obscure pre-war Prussian police detachment (at the time, Hermann Göring was Prussian Minister of the Interior). It was upgraded to a regiment in 1935 and transferred to the Luftwaffe in October of that year. Enlarged once more, this time to brigade size in July 1942, within just three months it had increased in size again to divisional status.

Panzer Regiment *Hermann Göring* was formed in April 1943 and shortly thereafter the division itself was accorded Panzer division status. By the end of the war, further expansion had seen the creation of Fallschirmpanzer Korps consisting of Fallschirm Panzer Division 1 *Hermann Göring* and Fallschirm Panzergrenadier Division 2 *Hermann Göring*. Recruitment was from the whole of Germany, and as well as the normal eligibility criteria, those applying to serve in the *Hermann Göring* Division had to guarantee that they would eternally support the National Socialist state. Recruits entering the *Hermann Göring* Division benefited from being quartered in a brand new, purpose built barracks at Berlin-Reinickendorf, lavishly equipped with the latest amenities including modern gymnasium and indoor and outdoor swimming pools. For the greatest part of its life, the *Hermann Göring* Division accepted only the best recruits. In the latter part of the war, like most other units, it was required to accept whatever drafts of manpower became available.

Leibstandarte SS Adolf Hitler

This was *the* elite unit of the SS, and it had its origins in Hitler's personal bodyguard. By the outbreak of war in 1939 it had reached the status of a motorised infantry regiment and served in this capacity in the Polish campaign. It attained divisional size in November 1942, and it converted to Panzer division status in October 1943. The *Leibstandarte* recruited throughout Germany and only the highest quality candidates were accepted. Hitler is said to have insisted, 'My Leibstandarte will accept no one who is not the best that Germany can offer!' Recruits had to be at least 6ft 1½ ins tall, of the highest possible standards of physical fitness, of traceable Aryan ancestry back to 1800 for other ranks and 1750 for officers, no criminal record and even his physical features had to match Himmler's standards for Nordic appearance. Recruits signed on for four years in the ranks, extending to 12 years for NCOs and 25 for officers.

TRAINING

On receiving his call-up notice and reporting for duty, the prospective Panzer soldier underwent the basic military training common to all German soldiers. Most recruits had already been involved with the compulsory state labour programme or the Hitler Youth, so they generally came into the army with a better awareness of the realities of military life than recruits in other countries.

A typical German recruit would have already learned the significance of military rank structures and basic drill movements, he would be extremely fit and he would also be accustomed to wearing uniform.

Panzers on the training grounds. Although at first glance these rare vehicles look like Panzer IVs with eight roadwheels, they are in fact Panzer IIIbs, of which only 15 were built, in 1937. Later versions of the Panzer III had only six roadwheels. (Robert Noss)

Throughout all of the civil and paramilitary organisations of the Third Reich, sport was given the highest possible profile. As a result, recruits had a good standard of general fitness and could spend their time on military training rather than on PT. Nevertheless, basic military training would be no picnic. Basic training equipped the recruit for combat service and, in addition to familiar exercises such as drill movements and firearms training, exercises under live fire were widely used. In the German armed forces, unlike in many other armies, soldiers were encouraged to use their initiative; thus if an NCO or squad leader was killed or injured, a junior rank would have the skills and confidence required to take over.

Even for tank crews, basic infantry training was essential. If a vehicle was knocked out or disabled, the crew would have to fend for themselves, and in the event, many of them did so admirably. Photographs show a surprisingly large number of Panzer soldiers wearing the Close Combat Clasp, awarded for hand-to-hand fighting.

On completion of his basic infantry training, the recruit commenced specialist Panzer training. From the beginning, Guderian had favoured highly structured training. First the individual would receive his own training, then the various crew members would come together and exercise as a team. Trained crews would take part in unit level exercises and finally the units themselves would be involved in large-scale manoeuvres.

Guderian had immersed himself in studying tank tactics during the 1920s, and in 1931, having been given command of 3. *Kraftfahrabteilung* in Berlin, he set about putting his theories into practice. His transport unit made dummy hardboard superstructures that were fitted over the bodies of light cars to give the appearance of a tank. As a result, by the time the first Panzer Mk Is rolled off the production lines, training of tank crews, at least in tactical exercises, was already underway.

Finally, in November 1933, Panzer training proper began, with the establishment of a new training school, the Panzertruppen-Schule at Wunsdorf-Zossen. The school was eventually split to form two new schools: Panzerschule 1 at Bergen, which specialised in training tank and anti-tank personnel; and Panzerschule 2 at Potsdam-Krampnitz, where Panzer grenadiers and Panzer reconnaissance troops were trained. In addition to basic tank training, specialisation courses were run for Panther crews at Erlangen training grounds and Tiger crews at Paderborn training grounds. For most of the war, NCO training for tank crews was carried out by the Feld-Unteroffizier-Schule near Warsaw in occupied Poland.

Officer candidate training was the responsibility of the

The front cover of the *Tigerfibel*, the training manual for the legendary Tiger tank.

Fahnenjunker-Schule der Panzertruppen at Gross-Glienicke near Berlin, and specific courses were run at Panzer training establishments at Gross-Glienicke, Ohrdruf and Wischau. Advanced officer candidate training was also carried out at Gross-Glienicke and Wischau by the Oberfähnrich-Schule der Panzertruppe.

Tank commanders were selected from the best of the trained tank crews, and in turn the *Zugführer* (troop leader) would be selected from the best of the commanders.

At the outbreak of the Spanish Civil War, Germany dispatched a number of its light 5-ton Panzerkampfwagen Is to support the Nationalist cause. Although the German personnel who accompanied the tanks were intended to train Spanish crews for the tanks rather than crew them themselves, once the training had been completed, the German crews were also permitted to go into action. Thus the Panzerwaffe, in the days leading up to the outbreak of the Second World War, had the priceless opportunity to test themselves, their tactics and their vehicles in action. They learned many valuable lessons in the process.

In September 1937, the first large-scale tank training manoeuvres were held around Neustrelitz in front of a high-ranking audience, which included the Italian dictator Mussolini. By the outbreak of war, it was clear to the Germans that their Mk I and Mk II Panzers were hopelessly under-gunned, the former having only machine guns and the latter only a 2-cm cannon. Nevertheless, these vehicles would form the backbone of the *Panzerwaffe* during the attack on Poland.

More suitable for modern warfare were the Panzer III at 20 tons, and the Panzer IV at 25 tons. The Panzer III was the more numerous, though it had only a 5-cm gun. The heavier Panzer IV with its short-barrelled 7.5-cm gun was intended for the infantry support role, though it would later develop into a fine medium tank and the most numerous of all types of Panzer. It soon became clear that in many ways, the Panzer crew closely resembled the crew of a U-boat. A small team, each dependent on his crewmates, fighting within an enclosed steel environment. As with the U-boats, it was essential that each Panzer crewman had a working knowledge of the skills required for each job within the crew in case one of his comrades was killed or injured. The loss of any one crewman (typically, medium tanks would have a crew of five) could seriously impair or even totally negate the tank's fighting ability if a colleague could not step in and fill the breach.

Specialist training

Initial driver training was given using cut-down examples of the Panzer I or Panzer II with the turret and superstructure removed. As well as the army's own instructors, considerable use was made of the facilities of the NSKK, the Party's own motor corps. Many period photographs show tanks on training exercises with the letters NSKK stencilled on the front glacis plate. Of course, prior to Germany's open rearmament, the country was prohibited from having tanks by the Treaty of Versailles, so the first Mk Is were designated as small tractors. But whether tanks or tractors, the important thing was that the trainee had the opportunity to learn the art of driving a tracked vehicle, something quite different to controlling a wheeled conveyance.

Gunnery training was undertaken at the ranges at Putlos on the Baltic. As the Panzerwaffe grew, so did the number of designated training schools and training areas. Many such sites, for example the Sennelager training area, are still in use today as Panzer training grounds.

As the war drew on, progress in tank technology was meteoric. Vehicles such as the Panther and Tiger were so complex (and because of this complexity, liable to mechanical failure) that special training was required. In each case a special training manual was produced. These excellent books, which resembled children's school text-books, were known as the *Tiger Fibel* or *Panther Fibel* (Tiger or Panther primers), and used coloured cartoon sketches to illustrate in the clearest possible fashion how particular tasks should be performed.

The most important part of Panzer training, apart from the technical training on how to operate the vehicle itself, was on how to use the tank as an efficient fighting weapon. Again a training circular was produced, based on combat experience on the Eastern Front, and like the Fibels, it was published in a simple cartoon format. It laid down 30 rules and was aimed primarily at junior officer level. What follows is not an exact translation, but a summary of the salient points.

1 Acquaint yourself with the terrain, and share this information with subordinates.
2 Always put subordinates 'in the picture' about the tactical situation, the mission and any other relevant information.
3 Protect your flanks as well as your front.
4 Always make constant appreciation of the changing situation.
5 Maintain strict radio discipline.
6 Lead with strength! At least two Panzers forward. The more firepower that is laid down in the first minute, the faster the enemy will be defeated.
7 When breaking from cover do so quickly and in unison. The more targets the enemy is faced with at one time, the more difficult it will be for him to control his fire, and you will have all the more firepower available to strike him.
8 During an attack, move as fast as possible. You are much more likely to be hit at slow speed. There are only two speeds – slow for firing, and full speed ahead.
9 When facing anti-tank weapons at long or medium distance, first return fire before moving against them. First, halt to return fire effectively, then commit the bulk of the company to move against them whilst leaving one platoon to give supporting fire.
10 If anti-tank weapons are encountered at close range, it is suicide to stop! Only immediate aggressive attack at full speed and with all guns firing can be successful and reduce losses.
11 In action against anti-tank guns, never allow a single platoon to attack alone, even with strong covering fire. Anti-tank guns are not deployed singly. Remember, lone tanks in Russia are lost!
12 Keep a good distance between vehicles. This divides the enemy's defensive fire. Avoid narrow gaps between vehicles at all costs.
13 If an impassable obstacle such as a minefield or ditch is met, withdraw into cover immediately. Standing still in the open will cost you losses. Make your deliberations from the safety of cover.

14 If passing potential enemy tank positions, either pass so close that you are within their minimum range, or so far as to be outside their maximum range.

15 Do not attack enemy tanks directly, they will then know your strength and respond before you can kill them. Wait until you are in a favourable position and attack from the flanks or the rear. Pursue all retreating enemy vigorously.

16 An enemy strongpoint should be attacked from different directions simultaneously if possible. Defensive fire will be split and the true source and direction of your attack concealed. Your breakthrough will be easier and your casualties fewer.

17 Always prepare dug-in positions and camouflage against air or artillery attacks. There is no excuse for losses suffered through these causes.

18 In decisive moments, do not try to conserve ammunition. At such times it is acceptable to expend ammunition at exceptionally high rates to minimise casualties.

19 Never deploy your company in such a manner that the two parts cannot support each other. If there are two objectives, attack each in turn with your full strength.

20 Make use of supporting artillery or dive-bomber attacks immediately. Do not wait until such attacks cease. They only have suppressive, not destructive effect. It is better to risk friendly fire than rush into an active anti-tank defence.

21 Do not misuse attached arms. For instance do not use engineer troops as infantry, armoured infantry in place of tanks.

22 Protect any non-armoured or lightly armoured units attached to you from unnecessary losses until they are needed for the task for which they were attached.

23 Attached units are not your servants but your guests. Supply them with their needs and share with them. Do not just use them for guard duties!

Having returned from the front, these Panzer crewmen from 2. SS Panzer Regiment *Das Reich* pose in front of their factory fresh Panzer IV with the long-barrelled 7.5-cm gun. Note the vehicle to the left still has the earlier short-barrelled version of this weapon. (Robert Noss)

A Panzer company line up for inspection. The photograph was probably taken in 1943; the year in which the M1943 Einheitsfeldmütze, worn by the officer taking the salute, was introduced. By the following year, the Panzer III, just visible at the end of the rows of black uniformed tank crewmen, would have been largely replaced by the Panzer IV or Panther. (Robert Noss)

24 In combined operations, work closely together and help each other. Your battle cry will be 'Protect the Infantry!' and theirs will be 'Protect the Panzers!'

25 Always concentrate on your mission and do not be diverted into attacking enemy flanking positions unless they threaten accomplishment of your mission.

26 After a victory, always be prepared for a counter-attack.

27 In defensive positions, leave only a few Panzers in static firing positions. Keep the remainder mobile so that they can be brought into play quickly and effectively. Tanks should defend aggressively.

28 In meeting exceptionally strong resistance, break off the attack. Continuing only costs more casualties. It is better to hold the enemy with minimal forces whilst you mass your strength for a surprise attack from another quarter.

29 Never forget. Your soldiers are not yours, but Germany's. Glory hunting only rarely succeeds but always costs blood. Temper your courage with judgement and cunning. Use your instincts and tactical ability. You will then earn the loyalty and respect of your soldiers.

30 The Panzer division is the modern equivalent of the cavalry. Panzer officers must carry on the cavalry traditions and its aggressive spirit. Remember the motto of Marshal Blucher: 'Forwards and through' (but sensibly).

APPEARANCE

Panzertruppe were unusual among German troops in that an exceptionally large range of special clothing was available to them. Far too much space would be required to describe each and every nuance of Panzertruppe clothing, so only a brief overview is given here. Fuller details of both uniforms and insignia may be found in several of the books listed in the bibliography. Panzertruppe uniforms may be considered under the following basic headings: parade dress; service dress; special panzer clothing; working dress; and camouflaged dress.

Parade dress

Typical parade dress for Panzer troops consisted of the so-called *Waffenrock* tunic with piped trousers and steel helmet. The Waffenrock was a single-breasted, pocketless tunic with Swedish cuffs. It was cut from fine, field grey wool, with a contrasting, dark green woollen badge-cloth collar. The front opening of the tunic, the collar and cuffs were piped in rose pink, which was the branch of service colour of the Panzers.

The collar was adorned with aluminium braid bars called Litzen, which were mounted on a pink wool base. Smaller versions of these patches also featured on the cuff.

The rear vent of the jacket was decorated with three buttons each side and was also piped in pink. On the left breast was affixed a national emblem, either machine-woven or hand-embroidered in aluminium wire. Officer and lower-rank tunics were similar but differed in the heavier, higher quality insignia worn by officers. For NCO ranks, the upper edge and front of the collar, and the edges of the cuff patches, were trimmed with flat aluminium wire tresse.

Shoulder straps were dark green wool for lower ranks, piped in pink and with the regimental number embroidered in pink thread. NCO straps had the same braid trim as the collar. Officer straps were in bright aluminium braid on a pink underlay, and they carried the regimental number in gilt metal.

Trousers were cut from stone grey wool, were straight legged and worn tucked into jackboots. Trouser seams were piped in pink.

Even bandsmen within Panzer units wore the black uniform wherever possible. Here a trombonist from 1. SS Panzer Division *Leibstandarte SS Adolf Hitler* plays from a selection of Luftwaffe marches. (Josef Charita)

A scene from the funeral of Generalmajor Landgraf. A Panzer V 'Panther', in this case an early model D, escorts the coffin to its final resting place as the band standing under the trees to the left plays the mournful 'Ich hatte einen Kameraden'. (Robert Noss)

The steel helmet was normally worn with parade dress, although officers sometimes wore the peaked service cap. Lower ranks wore a plain, black leather belt with aluminium or silvered finish buckle, whilst officers wore a silver brocade belt, which was trimmed in green, with a circular aluminium buckle.

Manufacture of this form of dress was discontinued upon the outbreak of war.

Service dress

Basic service dress worn by Panzertruppe when not serving in the armoured vehicle, was the universal, four-pocket, field grey wool tunic and trousers. It was a uniform worn by all army troops, and only the pink piping to collar patches and shoulder straps and to the peaked service cap, indicated the wearer's membership of the Panzerwaffe. In this case, lower ranks generally wore a black leather waistbelt, which was adorned by a steel buckle that was painted dark green. Officers wore a black leather belt with a plain, double-claw buckle.

Panzertruppe serving in warm regions such as North Africa and Italy usually wore the lightweight, olive denim four-pocket tropical tunic. Alternatively, they might resort to wearing shirtsleeve order, even when in their armoured vehicles, rather than adopt the special, black panzer clothing. Panzer troops wore the small metal death's-head emblem from the collar patch of the black Panzer jacket, on the lower lapel facings of the tropical jacket. Both the tropical field cap and the peaked tropical field cap may be found with the national colours cockade enclosed within an inverted soutache of Panzer pink piping. However, using the tank's sighting periscopes whilst wearing a cap with a long visor was difficult, and so most tank crews used the visorless field cap.

Special Panzer clothing

A smart and functional special form of dress was introduced for tank crews in 1934. It consisted of a waist-length, double-breasted jacket that was cut from black wool. The jacket was pocketless on the exterior (an interior pocket was normally provided) and had concealed buttons. It was worn in conjunction with black trousers, bloused at the ankle, and short black boots. Although a matching black field cap (and ultimately a black ski cap) was produced, due to shortages of the correct headgear in the early part of the war, the field grey version of the cap was often worn with black Panzer clothing (*Panzerbekleidung*).

In the early months of the war, some troops were still wearing the Panzer beret. This large, floppy, wool beret, which was worn pulled over a padded, leather-framed crash helmet, was rarely seen by 1940.

The Panzer jacket originally featured pink piping around the collar (removed in later jackets) and pink-piped, black wool shoulder straps. NCO versions had the traditional *Tresse* (braid) edging to the shoulder strap, but unlike other forms of jacket, no NCO tresse was featured on the collar. Officers' shoulder straps were in matt aluminium braid on a pink underlay. Collar patches were identical for all ranks and

A *fahnenjuncker oberfeldwebel* (officer candidate) in black Panzer dress. The wearing of officer chin-cords on his peaked cap indicates his status. In his lapel buttonhole is the ribbon of the Iron Cross Second Class, and on his left breast the Panzer Assault Badge and Wound Badge. He also wears the ribbon of the East Front Medal. (Robert Noss)

A Panzer hauptmann in the cupola of his Panzer IV. He wears the popular black version of the officer's field cap and the green denim, lightweight version of the Panzer jacket. Note also the headset and throat microphone being worn. (Robert Noss)

consisted of a parallelogram of black wool, piped in pink, with a small, silvered metal death's head in the centre.

The national emblem was worn on the left breast from 1935 onwards (prior to this date no national emblem was worn on the Panzer jacket or Panzer beret) and it came in several variations. It could be in machine woven white thread on black; grey thread on black; aluminium thread on black; or, on some officer jackets, hand-embroidered aluminium thread on black.

Those units granted authority to wear a cuffband with their unit name wore it on the lower part of the right sleeve. For a short period, Panzer pioneers wore black and white twist piping instead of pink. Armoured cavalry units also wore black Panzer clothing but with golden yellow piping.

The black field cap featured a grey, white or aluminium woven national emblem on black, over a national colours cockade, which was also displayed on black backing. Early caps had the cockade enclosed by an inverted soutache of pink piping, while officers' caps featured silver piping along the edge of the crown and front scalloped portion of the cap flap.

The later M1943 Einheitsfeldmütze field cap featured flaps at the side that buttoned (either with one or, more commonly, two buttons) at the front of the cap. These flaps could be folded down during cold periods to give protection to the wearer's ears and to the side and rear of his head. Though popular, this cap featured a peak that prevented easy use of the periscope visor sights in the tank's interior, so the cap can sometimes be seen being worn back to front. The special Panzer clothing was also manufactured in lightweight green denim for wear in summer months; this version had a large exterior patch pocket to the left breast.

Even the German police issued their armoured troops with a special version of the black Panzer clothing (the collar was piped in Polizei green) with appropriate police insignia. This form of dress was worn by police security units that had been issued with obsolete or captured armoured vehicles.

Working dress

A one-piece boiler suit garment was also produced for armoured vehicle crews. It could be worn over the black Panzer clothing or its lightweight denim summer equivalent. Generally no insignia was worn on this apparel, and it was often used when employed on messy maintenance work in an effort to keep the Panzer clothing in decent condition. It was also used in winter months, to add another layer of clothing in an effort to keep warm.

Camouflage dress

A special version of the Panzer clothing was also manufactured, though in very small numbers, in camouflage material bearing a splinter pattern as used on the German Army's camouflaged shelter quarter (the 'Poncho' or 'Zeltbahn'). Insignia was not always worn with camouflage clothing, but when it was used, it was often restricted to shoulder straps only. A splinter camouflage version of the M1943 field cap was also produced in limited numbers; possibly manufactured by unit tailors using the material from surplus Zeltbahns.

A Panzerschütze wearing the black Panzer uniform as walking-out dress with white shirt and black tie. Although against regulations, this practice was widespread. His black wool shoulder straps show a pink thread embroidered 'GD' monogram for Panzer Regiment *Grossdeutschland*.

Uniforms of non-army Panzer units

In addition to the army Panzer units, which formed the vast bulk of the Panzerwaffe, both Waffen-SS and Luftwaffe troops also served in tank units. Though their uniforms were very similar to that of the army, there were some differences worth commenting upon.

Luftwaffe

The *Hermann Göring* Panzer Division of the Luftwaffe used black Panzer clothing identical in cut to that of the army. Collars and collar patches were piped, however, in white (sometimes in silver twist cord for officers), and the national emblem worn on the left breast was of the Luftwaffe's stylised flying eagle. Later, standard type Luftwaffe *Hermann Göring* white collar patches were used, but with the Panzer death's head attached rather than the normal gull wing insignia of the Luftwaffe. These white patches were sometimes piped in aluminium twist cord. A black field cap, similar to the navy's, which lacked the scalloped front to the flap, was used, as was a black M1934 Einheitsfeldmütze. Once again, the national emblem used was the Luftwaffe flying eagle, but this time it was on a black backing.

Luftwaffe Panzer troops wore the standard blue-grey Luftwaffe (four-pocket tunic) or the smart, but functional, Fliegerbluse (fliers jacket) when they were not wearing special Panzer clothing.

Waffen-SS

The Waffen-SS used a Panzer jacket of slightly different cut to that of the army. The front flap was cut vertically, rather than slanting as on the army's, and the collar was of a smaller, neater cut. The Waffen-SS also used surplus army stock as well as their own distinct pattern.

No piping was worn on the collar of the Waffen-SS tunic for lower ranks, but officers wore piping in twisted aluminium cord. Standard Waffen-SS collar patches were worn as used on Waffen-SS field grey clothing. There were no special Panzer tabs, though some units did attach pink piping to the standard Waffen-SS tabs for NCO and lower ranks.

The standard Waffen-SS sleeve eagle was worn on the left sleeve, woven in grey, white or aluminium thread or hand embroidered in aluminium wire.

Straps were cut from black wool for lower ranks, with tresse for NCOs. Officers' straps were in matt aluminium, with a pink intermediate piping, all on a black wool base. Those units granted authority to wear a cuffband bearing the unit name wore it on the lower left sleeve.

The black Feldmütze and black M1943 Einheitsfeldmütze worn by the Waffen-SS was identical to the Luftwaffe pattern. For officers, silver piping was worn to the flap of the Feldmütze and to the crown of the Einheitsfeldmütze. The national emblem worn was the SS pattern, and the SS death's head was worn in place of the national colours cockade.

Waffen-SS units also used a camouflaged version of the Panzer clothing, which was cut in lightweight denim in so-called 'pea pattern' camouflage. Although only shoulder straps were to be worn on this

The special black Panzer version of the M1943 Einheitsfeldmütze. The insignia is that worn by the Waffen-SS, with the death's head on the front of the cap and the SS version of the national emblem on the left side flap.

Members of the armoured recce unit of the *Leibstandarte SS Adolf Hitler* during the Polish Campaign. They wear the early Panzer beret. Of particular interest is the fact that field grey cloth patches have been sewn over the top of their collar patches. Although not visible in this shot, other photographs from the same series show that unit cuffbands were similarly concealed. (Gary Wood)

tunic, it was also often seen with the sleeve eagle attached. Trousers in identical camouflage pattern were worn with the jacket. Waffen-SS units also made wide use of a one-piece boiler suit in a similar camouflage pattern. This was rarely worn with insignia other than occasional straps.

Waffen-SS tank troops were unique in making widespread use of leather clothing; much of which was surplus navy engine room crew clothing. The shortish black leather, single-breasted jacket was particularly popular. They were blanket-lined to give extra warmth in winter, and the leather gave an element of protection against burns, an occupational hazard for tank men. The only insignia normally worn with this form of clothing was the shoulder strap.

Of all the uniform types worn by the Panzertruppe, the special black clothing was by far the most popular. Though strictly speaking it was only intended for wear when serving in the armoured vehicle, it was so well liked that it was widely worn as walking-out dress. Given the smart, elegant appearance of this black clothing it is not surprising that it was

A group of Panzer crewmen from the *Leibstandarte SS Adolf Hitler*. Note that the NCO on the left wears the full two-piece camouflaged version of the Panzer uniform, but with the field grey, not black, Feldmütze. No shirt is worn. The SS-Oberscharführer to his right wears the jacket buttoned up to the neck, a less common practice. The centre figure wears the mouse grey shirt. Once again, the two crewmen, at right, have elected to wear the camouflaged Panzer uniform, one with the collar buttoned up and the other with it opened, in this case with the mouse grey shirt worn underneath. The crewman, second from right, has the single-button version of the M1943 Einheitsfeldmütze. The senior NCO, second from left, wears the metal version of the unit's 'LAH' monogram on his shoulder straps, whilst the SS-Unterscharführer, second from right, wears his in embroidered form on a separate cloth slide. SS-Unterscharführer Horst Schumann, at extreme right, wears straps with the monogram embroidered directly onto them. This shot can be considered typical of the appearance of an SS tank crew from 1943 through to the end of the war. (Schumann)

The five-man crew of a Panzer III from an SS Panzer regiment. Only the driver wears the black Panzer jacket, the remainder of the crew being in shirtsleeve order. Of interest is the special sleeve rank insignia, intended for wear on garments without shoulder straps. These, for non-officer ranks, consisted of a simple system of green horizontal bars on a black backing. (Robert Noss)

so popular. In cold weather, the standard field grey wool (field blue for the Luftwaffe) greatcoat could be worn over the black Panzer clothing, though this cumbersome garment was not ideal apparel for the close confines of a tank.

Later in the war, padded winter parkas became available, and there is no shortage of photographic evidence of these being worn by tank crews. Though still cumbersome and bulky, they were far less awkward than the greatcoat, and considerably warmer.

Strangely, whether army, Luftwaffe or Waffen-SS, few tank crewmen adhered to any standard form of dress where shirts were concerned. Regulation mouse grey shirts were often worn with the black Panzer jacket, as were non-regulation white shirts, v-necked, grey wool jumpers or roll-neck sweaters. As, technically, the Panzer jacket was only supposed to be worn when serving in the tank, and not when in barracks or on leave, it was probably felt acceptable to allow crews to wear whatever they were most comfortable with under active service conditions.

ACTIVE SERVICE

Pay

The pay scales for Panzer soldiers were the same as for all other troops. Unlike U-boat crews, they were not accorded a special additional rate of pay, though Panzer troops serving in North Africa did receive a pay addition; the so-called *Afrika-Zulage*. Soldiers on front-line combat duties were rewarded with the *Frontzulage* (front-line supplement).

Ranks

Rank structure for Panzer soldiers was identical to that for other non-armoured troops. In the case of privates, however, the rank of 'schütze' should be prefixed by 'Panzer'. Although the private was a Panzerschütze, as soon as he received his first stripe, he became a simple 'gefreiter' (lance-corporal) as with all other branches, the 'Panzer' prefix was dropped. The Panzer crew was usually a mixture of privates and junior NCO ranks, the individual tank commanders were more likely to be junior or senior sergeant equivalents and the troop commanders were warrant officer or junior commissioned officer ranks.

The Panzer crew

As previously mentioned, there were a number of similarities between service in Panzers and service in U-boats. In both cases, a relatively small crew served within a small, claustrophobic and often thoroughly unpleasant environment, where the survival of each crew member depended on not only him carrying out his allotted tasks swiftly and efficiently, but also upon his crewmates doing likewise. In both cases, the vessel or vehicle was a highly potent war machine, which had the potential to wreak havoc upon the enemy, but should it receive a direct hit from enemy fire, the chances of survival for any of the crew were slim. In both services, the death rate amongst crews was extremely high.

A typical five-man crew comprised: driver; radio-operator/machine gunner; gunner; loader; and commander.

The driver (*fahrer*) sat in the forward left side of the hull and steered the tank by a combination of steering levers, a steering wheel or both. Foot pedals operated the tank's clutch, accelerator and brakes. The driver's seat could be raised or lowered so that he could drive with his

An SS-Unterscharführer cleans the muzzle brake of his vehicle's main armament. He wears the SS version of the black Panzer Feldmütze. Note that around the death's-head insignia is an inverted chevron of pink Panzer piping. His work jacket bears only shoulder straps; collar patches and sleeve eagles rarely if ever being worn on this dress. (Gary Wood)

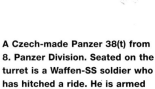

A Czech-made Panzer 38(t) from 8. Panzer Division. Seated on the turret is a Waffen-SS soldier who has hitched a ride. He is armed with a captured Soviet PPsH machine pistol, much prized by German troops. Note that two of the tank crew still wear the older field grey version of the Feldmütze. (Robert Noss)

An exhausted tank crewman snatches some overdue sleep in a rather unusual spot, lying atop the running gear of his Panzer III. (Robert Noss)

head out of the hatch in safe areas, thereby enjoying better vision. When the hatch was battened down for action, the driver's only source of vision was a narrow view port or episcope sight, making controlling and steering the tank an exhausting task and often requiring guidance from the commander, who benefited from a superior viewing position.

To the right of the forward hull compartment sat the radio operator (*funker*), who also manned the hull machine gun. The radio operator could lay down suppressive fire to prevent any enemy infantry closing near enough to become a threat to the vehicle.

In the turret, to the right, sat the loader (*ladeschütze*), whose job was to serve the main gun with ammunition. Loading could be a back-breaking task, manhandling heavy shells in the close confines of the turret. The shells were stored in racks, some of which were awkward to access during combat. The loader was also responsible for making sure that the correct type of ammunition was loaded. A high-explosive shell fired at an enemy heavy tank, for example, would probably do no more than give the opposing crew a headache. Similarly, an armour-piercing shell fired at enemy trenches would do little damage unless it scored a direct hit, and even then, the damage would be confined to the point of impact. The loader also maintained the co-axial turret machine-gun, ensuring sufficient ammunition was loaded. To the left of the turret interior sat the gun-layer (*richtschütze*), who aimed and fired the main gun, on the commander's orders. Sighting was through binocular or monocular sights.

In order to cope with the snow-covered Russian winter terrain, tanks were fitted with so-called 'Ost-Ketten' or 'Eastern Tracks' – specially extended track links. These can be seen to best effect where the track loops over the rear idler wheel. (Robert Noss)

A rare Panzer IIIb, identified by its eight roadwheels, during the Polish campaign. In this period, the insignia carried on German armoured vehicles was a plain white cross; this of course presented a perfect aiming point for enemy gunners and was quickly replaced by the well-known black cross with white edges. (Robert Noss)

At the rear of the turret sat the commander. At safe distances, he would stand on his small seat, so that his upper body was exposed in the cupola, and observe the battlefield with binoculars. When the enemy was near and in combat situations the turret hatch was battened down, and the commander observed the battlefield through small episcopes set into the cupola surface.

Tank crews were supplied with headsets and throat microphones so that orders could be heard clearly over the noise of the gun and the tank's engine and machinery. An electrical switch usually fired the main armament. The gunner also operated the co-axial machine gun, usually by a foot pedal.

During the second half of the war, many tanks had provision for an additional machine gun to be fitted on a special circular mount welded to the commander's cupola. From wartime photographs it seems that this weapon was not regularly fitted. To use it, the commander would have had to expose most of his upper body to enemy return fire.

Even at the best of times, tanks were never comfortable vehicles. In summer, the effect of serving in a steel box on the Russian Steppe or in the desert would be somewhat akin to being baked in an oven. For safety's sake the hatch had to be battened down if the enemy was nearby, since a grenade lobbed inside or a stray bullet could have devastating effect, so barely a breath of fresh air was available. In battle conditions, the ventilator fans would also struggle to extract the cordite fumes as the main armament was fired. Sweating and choking, many tank crews served dressed only in shorts and canvas shoes. In dusty or sandy areas, air filters would clog and particles would be drawn into the engine, scouring the cylinders and drastically reducing the effective life of the engine.

In winter, and in particular in the first half of the war, when purpose-designed winter clothing had yet to be introduced, tank crews were reduced to wearing the bulky wool greatcoat from the field grey uniform. The greatcoat was far from ideal, making movement difficult in the already cramped confines of the tank. If summer in a tank was akin to being baked in an oven, then winter could be compared to life in a freezer; since the heat from the tank's engines was totally inadequate against the cold.

In extreme conditions on the Eastern Front, lubricating oil would freeze, thereby immobilising engines and transmission systems. In some cases crews had to resort to building fires under their vehicles in an attempt to thaw out the engines. Snow would often build up in the space between the hull and tracks, becoming hard packed and often causing a track to be 'thrown' (the track being dislodged from the toothed drive sprocket). If this happened when a tank was under fire, it could have fatal consequences.

The headset and throat microphone systems that were issued to crews also caused unique problems. Although such devices made communication possible in the noisy environs of the tank, the wearing of the unit's bulky headphones precluded the use of a steel helmet, so when the commander stood in his hatch, his head was vulnerable to shell splinters and shrapnel. A new system was introduced in 1944 with the headphones set lower to allow a helmet to be worn. Somewhat perversely, however, these units were introduced only after the issue of steel helmets to tank crews had ceased.

Tanks are built as fighting machines, not limousines, so the interiors are spartan, with few comforts for the crews, but many awkward, protruding pieces of equipment to painfully knock parts of the body against as the tank trundles over rough, uneven ground. But during the Second World War, tanks were not only uncomfortable but also prone to mechanical breakdown. These heavy machines were, wherever possible, transported by rail, but sometimes had to travel considerable distances over land. In such conditions, transmissions failed, tracks broke and engines seized up with alarming regularity.

German tanks were well engineered, sometimes over-engineered compared with the crudely made but effective Soviet T34 for example,

A Panzer III on the Eastern Front. Note how, like many tanks on active service, it has become covered with a clutter of jerricans, steel helmets and tarpaulin-covered stowage. (Robert Noss)

but they were not without their problems. Many were rushed through the development stages in a desperate effort to get them into action, and so took unresolved teething problems to the front with them. In addition, German tanks from the second half of the war, such as the Panther, Tiger and King Tiger, were extremely heavy and their power plants were only just up to the job of moving them. Routes had to be carefully chosen as many bridges could not support the weight of the heaviest vehicles. As the photographs in this book reveal, much time was spent on running repairs and maintenance.

A recovered Panzer III. Such vehicles, even if no longer fit for service, would be cannibalised for valuable spare parts. (Robert Noss)

MOTIVATION AND MORALE

Camaraderie and unit pride

In a similar vein to the situation on U-boats, good commanders had a strong bond with their crew members and treated them well. To have a sense of belief and belonging was a very strong motivator for the Panzertruppe. As with most armies, tank units tended to have strong links with the old cavalry, since it was usually the mechanisation of cavalry units that provided the first armoured regiments.

The choice of the death's-head emblem for the collar patch was a deliberate and logical choice, reinforcing the traditional links with the cavalry, amongst whom the 'Death or Glory' badge of the death's head was widely worn. The design of the black Panzer uniform itself was no accident. It was comfortable and functional for wear within the close confines of a

A Panzer crewman, flanked by two comrades, wears the black uniform for his wedding ceremony. It would be difficult to exaggerate the pride with which the black uniform was worn, and its contribution to the morale and *esprit de corps* of these elite troops. Strictly speaking, the soldier should be wearing his standard field grey uniform when on leave. (Robert Noss)

tank. Its colour was both stylish and useful for concealing oil or grease marks picked up from the tank's internal mechanisms, and the double-breasted cut and death's-head insignia harked back to the Uhlans

Unlike allied armies, which at the start of the Second World War saw the tank as predominantly a support weapon for the infantry, the Germans used the tank as a spearhead weapon. The pride of Panzer men in their branch of the armed forces was immense. The Blitzkrieg years saw German Panzers smash their way through every obstacle placed in their path. The newsreel films, watched by eager cinema audiences, invariably showed the overwhelming might of the Panzerwaffe as a regular theme. It is no surprise then that there was never a shortage of willing recruits for the Panzerwaffe.

In addition to the units that were formed as Panzer units, many of Germany's most prestigious units converted, first to Panzer grenadier (armoured infantry) then to full Panzer status as the war progressed. The pride of the German armed forces, the 'Grossdeutschland', developed from being a small but elite guard battalion to full Panzerkorps status. Hermann Göring, never one to allow his Luftwaffe to be outshone by others arms, ensured his own *Hermann Göring* Division was provided with a tank element, eventually becoming entitled, rather bizarrely, Fallschirmpanzerkorps (parachute armoured corps) *Hermann Göring*.

It was probably, however, the elite divisions of the Waffen-SS that gained the greatest fame, or notoriety, as Panzer divisions. A total of seven Waffen-SS divisions were either established as, or converted to, Panzer division

Cuffbands of the elite Panzer units of the Wehrmacht. At top is the silver wire on black, hand-embroidered *Grossdeutschland* cuffband in its distinctive Sütterlin script. In the centre is the silver wire on brown rayon woven band as worn by *Feldherrnhalle* units, and at bottom is the machine-embroidered enlisted ranks version in grey on black worn by Panzer personnel from the *Herrmann Göring* Division.

status. It has often been suggested that Waffen-SS divisions were given unfair priority in re-equipping with the latest, improved versions of various armoured vehicles. There is, however, little evidence to support this theory, as elite army units such as *Grossdeutschland* were also equipped with the best tanks available. It is more likely that the best equipment available was given first to those units that would make best use of it, i.e. those that were the most aggressive and daring in the attack and most tenacious in defence, and the Waffen-SS Panzer divisions certainly qualified on both counts.

Many of the Panzer units of the army adopted special unofficial unit insignia, which was worn on the side of the headgear in the same manner as the 'tradition' badges worn by U-boat crews. Probably the best known of these is the running greyhound of the 116 *Windhund* Panzer Division, but there were many others. Some units also produced their own newspapers or periodicals to foster a sense of common identity and build morale.

Cuffbands

The significance of the cuffband to unit identity and morale cannot be over-emphasised, In some units, *Hitlerjugend* for example, the unit cuffband was not issued until men had proven themselves in battle, and was accompanied by an award document. If the Panzerwaffe itself was considered an elite force, then the cuffband on the black jacket

symbolised *the* elite within the elite. When, in the final stages of the war, Hitler believed the Waffen-SS Panzer Divisions *Adolf Hitler, Das Reich* and others had failed him in not trying hard enough during the offensive around Lake Balaton, he ordered them to remove their cuffbands as a sign of disgrace. It was an act that finally lost him the respect of many of his most dedicated Waffen-SS troopers and it was also an order that was widely ignored.

Many elite Panzer units were given honour titles and permitted to wear a cuffband with the unit name (on the lower right sleeve for the army and Luftwaffe and on the lower left sleeve for the Waffen-SS). For the army

Cuffbands of the Waffen-SS Panzer regiments. All of these are woven in silver or grey yarn on a black rayon base. Originals such as those shown here now fetch astonishingly high prices.

Panzer divisions, *Grossdeutschland* wore a black band edged in silver with the unit title embroidered in old German 'Sütterlin' script. *Feldherrnhalle* wore a similar band but on brown backing. The Luftwaffe's *Hermann Göring* Division wore the unit title embroidered in block script on a blue band, but a version on black was also produced in limited numbers.

Cuffbands worn by all Waffen-SS Panzer divisions were worked on a black band. For the *Leibstandarte SS Adolf Hitler* the letters were worked in Sütterlin script and for all the others in normal Latin script. Generally speaking where within a Panzer division there were elite regiments with their own honour titles, the Panzer regiment took the name of the division. For example, within 2. SS-Panzer Division *Das Reich* were the elite Regiments *Deutschland*, *Der Führer* and *Germania*, the Panzer Regiment wore the *Das Reich* cuffband. Conversely, within 11. Panzer Grenadier Division *Nordland*, the Panzer Abteilung *Hermann von Salza* had its own band.

An award document for the Panzer Assault Badge in silver. This example was awarded posthumously to a Waffen-SS tank crewman killed in action on the Eastern Front. The document is signed by the regimental commander, Jochen Peiper.

The Panzer Assault Badge

One major factor that helped create a sense of belonging for the Panzertroops was the Panzer Assault Badge. Generaloberst von Brauchitsch instituted the badge on 20 December 1939, and it was to be issued to those soldiers who had taken part in at least three separate armoured assaults on three different dates.

The badge consisted of a wreath of oakleaves topped by the eagle and swastika national emblem. In the centre, facing right, was a representation of a short barrelled Mk IV Panzer. The badge was in silver finish and was worn on the left breast of the tunic.

As the war progressed it became clear that the Panzer Assault Badge was no longer sufficient reward for many tank troops who had served in dozens of additional actions without further recognition. Accordingly, on 22 June 1943 two new versions were introduced. The first was very similar to the basic badge, but was assembled from two pieces with the tank being riveted to the surrounding wreath. The wreath remained silver but the tank was blackened. At the base was a small box bearing the number '25' or '50', signifying the number of engagements in which the wearer had participated. The second new type was larger and wider, featuring a gilt wreath and silvered tank with the number '75' or '100' at the base of the wreath.

A: Panzer crewman, prior to the outbreak of war, c.1939

A

B: Driver and gunnery training

C: Panzerkampfwagen PZKPFW III advancing at speed across the Russian steppe, summer 1941

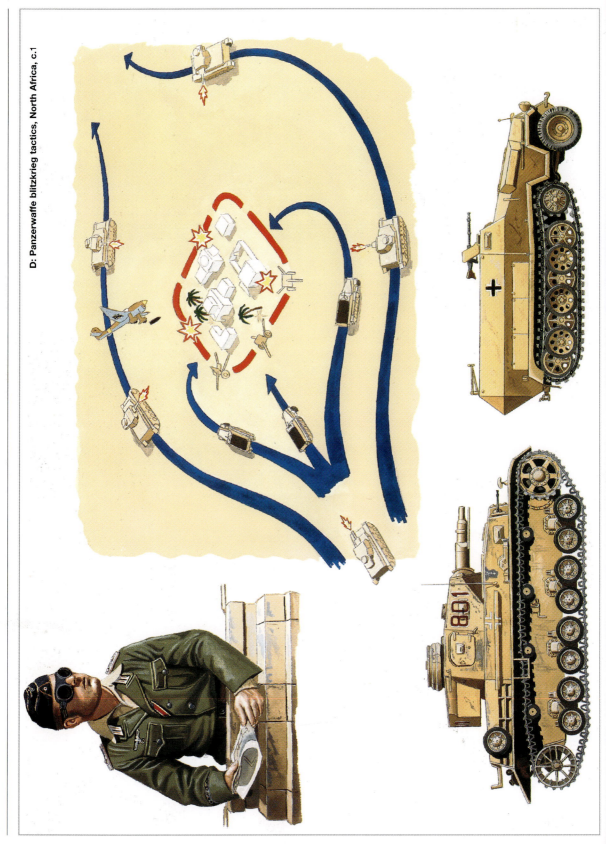

D: Panzerwaffe blitzkrieg tactics, North Africa, c.1

E: Tank maintenance

F: Panzerkampfwagen PZKPFWF Panther re-stocks with ammunition, Normandy, summer 1944

F

G: Feldwebel, of Panzer Regiment *Grossdeutschland*, c.1944

G

H: Panthers under allied air and artillery fire, 1945

Unit composition

The Panzerwaffe as a whole was a rather mixed bag. On one hand there were a considerable number of historic army units, steeped in a tradition going back to the times of the great Imperial cavalry regiments. On the other hand, there were the aggressive new Panzer divisions of the Waffen-SS, determined torchbearers of National Socialism and fanatically loyal to the State.

The Panzer Assault Badge in its basic form (left) awarded for participation in at least three separate actions, and (right) in the version awarded to those who had participated in at least 75 individual tank actions. Needless to say, the latter is extremely rare. (75 Panzer badge courtesy Mark Miller Collection)

The *Grossdeutschland* Division was unusual in that it recruited not from a specific region, but throughout Germany and was highly selective in whom it would accept. Applicants had to be of the highest standard of fitness but also of unquestionable loyalty. Indeed it was a unit of *Grossdeutschland* that eliminated the perpetrators of the July 1944 plot to assassinate Hitler. Nevertheless, *Grossdeutschland* fought with great elan, bravery and honour with no stains on its character or allegations of atrocities laid against it.

The Waffen-SS divisions of course represent a greyer area. There has never been any real dispute over the fighting qualities and almost reckless bravery of these elite troops. They, along with *Grossdeutschland*, were regularly used as a mobile 'fire brigade' on the Eastern Front, being rushed to wherever the next crisis arose. On the Western Front, the newly formed and untested young grenadiers of the *Hitlerjugend* fought the British and Canadians to a standstill at Caen in June 1944. Montgomery estimated that Caen would be captured on D-Day. Principally due to the fanatical endeavours of *Hitlerjugend*, Caen did not fall until 8 July, more than a month after D-Day.

The arrival of an SS Panzer unit equipped with even a handful of Tiger tanks on any sector of any front would almost certainly halt the enemy advance, if only temporarily.

The highest scoring tank aces of the Second World War were all from Waffen-SS Panzer units. Unfortunately however, many Waffen-SS units attracted an unsavoury reputation for brutality, much of it learned from their Soviet opponents on the battlefield. Despite this, Waffen-SS Panzer units such as *Hohenstaufen* and *Frundsberg* emerged from the war with a sound fighting reputation and very little to tarnish their name. *Frundsberg* and *Hohenstaufen* in particular fought most chivalrously against the Allied airborne landings at Arnhem and even the Soviets grudgingly accepted that *Wiking* was one of the best units they had ever faced.

It must be said that many of the young men who joined the Waffen-SS Panzer units during the Second World War were attracted to the glamorous uniforms and elite status of these units and did not share the Nazi politics of many of their comrades who had joined pre-war. Even the most hard-bitten veterans, however, had long lost their political ideals by the closing stages of the war and were no longer fighting for Hitler, but for the pride of their unit and the comrades they fought alongside. In the last few days of the war, when even the mightiest of the Panzer divisions were reduced to a handful of operational vehicles, their sense of pride in belonging to the Panzerwaffe remained undimmed.

DIVISIONAL ORGANISATION AND TACTICAL DEPLOYMENT

Before looking at specific Panzer combat actions, it is worth looking at the structure of a Panzer division. When Panzer divisions are mentioned, the first thing to come to mind is the tank, but the Panzer regiment around which a Panzer division was formed was only a small part of the whole. The make-up of Panzer divisions changed considerably throughout the war, so for the sake of simplicity what is considered in the following section is a 'typical' Panzer unit of 1944. By this time, a reasonable degree of standardisation had been achieved, although there could still be significant differences from one unit to another.

The central core of the Panzer division was, of course, the Panzer regiment. Typically it consisted of a headquarters element and two tank battalions. Each battalion consisted of four companies with, at full strength – which was in itself an unusual occurrence by 1944 – around 17 tanks each. Generally, in a well-equipped division, two of the four companies would be equipped with the Panzer IV and two with the powerful Panzer V Panther. Total regimental strength, including headquarters elements, would be around 155–159 tanks.

As well as the Panzer regiment itself, the typical Panzer division was equipped with a powerful Panzergrenadier regiment, which was split into two battalions, each of six companies. As well as basic armoured personnel carriers (usually the excellent SdKfz 251), the regiment would have numerous specialist vehicles based on the standard

A Panzer III in Russia, 1943. Note the additional track links placed over the frontal plates to give extra protection from enemy anti-tank guns. The crew's steel helmets have been slung from various suitable points on the tank's exterior, being too cumbersome to store within the tank. (Robert Noss)

armoured personnel carrier chassis, such as infantry support versions, flak versions and engineer versions.

Scouting ahead and protecting the division's flanks would be the *Panzeraufklärungsabteilung* (armoured reconnaissance detachment), equipped with motorcycles, light four-wheeled armoured cars and eight-wheeled heavy armoured cars.

Providing essential support in mine clearing, bridge building and obstacle demolition was the *Panzerpioniereabteilung* (armoured engineer detachment), which was equipped with numerous specialist vehicles based on half-tracked or fully tracked chassis.

Essential mobile fire support within a Panzer division was provided by the *Panzer Artillerie Abteilung*. These units were equipped with fully tracked, self-propelled artillery, usually of 10.5-cm or 15-cm calibre.

Defence of the division against enemy tanks was provided by the *Panzerjäger Abteilung* (tank hunter detachment). This element was armed with a range of specialist vehicles, usually based on conversions from existing Panzer chassis, and armed with high-velocity 7.5-cm or 8.8-cm guns.

Essential communications for the division were provided by the *Panzernachrichtenabteilung* (armoured signals detachment), which was responsible for both telephonic and radio signals, allocating call signs and monitoring enemy signals traffic.

An early Panzer IV on the Eastern Front. Note how the tracks have become clogged with mud. Crews took every chance to escape the noisy, hot interior of the tank and travel outside wherever safe to do so. (Robert Noss)

A Panzer IV halted for a brief rest on a muddy Soviet road. It can be assumed that the front line is still some way off, as the hull machine gun is still covered by its protective canvas sheath. (Robert Noss)

Some of the most important personnel within a Panzer division were the *Panzerinstandsetzungstruppen* (recovery and repair troops). The huge distances covered by tanks, especially on the Eastern Front, and the extremely difficult terrain crossed, meant that breakdowns were frequent. Recovery and repair troops ensured that, wherever possible, even under direct enemy fire, damaged tanks were recovered and captured enemy tanks were pressed into service. They were issued with the giant 'Famo' 18-ton half-tracks, as well as converted recovery versions of medium and heavy tanks such as the Panther.

Also of enormous importance were the *Nachschubtruppe* (divisional supply troops) who kept the Panzer division supplied with ammunition, food-fuel and other essentials. Smaller sub-units, such as the divisional military police troop, were often attached to this element.

Finally, it is worth looking at two small branches of the Panzerwaffe, which are rarely mentioned but nevertheless proudly wore the same special black Panzer uniforms as their more conventional comrades. Firstly, there were the *Eisenbahnpanzerzüge* (armoured railway trains). In some cases armoured trains were downgraded, non-mobile tanks, which were loaded on to special flatcars, and in others, were newly fabricated railway cars, fully armoured and fitted with tank turrets. Even less well known, were the few members of the *Panzer-Propagandatruppen*; these troops used armoured cars and small armoured half-tracks rather than tanks, but they wore the black Panzer uniform. Their duties included propaganda broadcasting, psychological warfare, and general reporting of front-line news. They were also responsible for the publication of soldiers' newspapers, specifically *Die Panzerfaust* (The Mailed Fist).

Waffen-SS tank crewmen assist in the re-ammunitioning of their early model Panther 'D'. They wear the reversible padded winter uniform with the white, snow camouflage side outwards, over their black Panzer uniforms. (Gary Wood)

With a full-strength Panzer division fielding up to 14,000 men, and the Panzer regiment itself having an average strength of some 800–1,000 tankers, it can be seen that the mighty Panzers themselves represented only a small part of the whole.

In addition to the Panzer divisions with their light and medium tanks, the mighty Tiger and King Tiger tanks were fielded in independent heavy tank battalions (*schwere Panzer Abteilungen*), which were attached at korps level and inserted into the front at crisis points. These Tiger battalions effectively became the korps' 'Fire Brigades', as did some of the better Panzer divisions themselves.

The Tigers, though immensely powerful, were slow and cumbersome and difficult to move. So wide was the Tiger, for instance, that it could not be transported by rail until its normal battle tracks had been replaced by narrower transport tracks. At its destination, the whole operation had to be repeated in reverse. As an attack weapon, therefore, the Tiger's success was limited. However, in defence, when the tank effectively served as a mobile blockhouse, they were devastating.

Extremely powerful tank destroyers were built on the chassis of the Panther (the *Jagdpanther*) and the King Tiger (the *Jagdtiger*) and formed into independent heavy tank-destroyer battalions

A Panther 'A' and its crew. The tank has been partially camouflaged with foliage, but the relaxed attitude of the crew suggests that there is no real threat of imminent enemy action. (Robert Noss)

A Waffen-SS Panther crew pose beside their immobilised vehicle. Note that the right-hand track is missing. However, there does not appear to be any damage to the vehicle. (Robert Noss)

(*schwere Panzerjäger Abteilungen*) attached at korps level. Although the *Jagdpanther* was a first-class vehicle and one of the best tank destroyers ever made, the *Jagdtiger* was a true behemoth. Weighing in at 77 tons and mounting a 12.8-cm gun, it could take out any other vehicle in existence, even at extreme range, but was itself so cumbersome and prone to breakdown that once spotted, it could be easily outflanked. Again, like the King Tiger, it was only effective as a defensive weapon. Tanks were generally used in two particular formations. Where a regimental-sized Kampfrgruppe was attacking, it would typically deploy a battalion-sized Panzer element, whose tank companies would adopt the famous *Panzerkeil* (tank-wedge), with the tanks moving in a 'V' or arrow formation. Alternatively units would employ the *Panzerglocke* (tank bell) with the heaviest Panzers, which constituted the 'clapper', surrounded by a screen of lighter tanks and armoured vehicles. The whole purpose of the tank, in Guderian's philosophy, was as a fast-moving breakthrough weapon, and not as some lumbering, slow-moving infantry support arm.

Panzers, upon meeting an obstacle such as a fortified town or village, simply divided and encircled the enemy in a pincer formation, bombarding them and subduing their positions, before leaving the 'mopping up' to the Panzergrenadiers. After the invasion of Russia, however, the opposition crumbled so fast that the Panzers ended up having to move equally fast in pursuit of the fleeing enemy and into the vastness of the Russian interior; their support, supplies and ammunition could barely keep pace.

Members of a Waffen-SS *Panzerinstandsetzung* unit unload a set of Panther tracks from a truck. Such units were kept extremely busy recovering and repairing damaged vehicles. (Robert Noss)

Panzers were often forced to halt and wait for the following infantry to catch up, otherwise they might be left deep in enemy territory without essential infantry support. After the Kursk offensive of 1943, the Panzers rarely had the opportunity to fulfil their role as an offensive weapon, but they proved themselves equally effective in defence, especially after the advent of the Tiger, *Königstiger*, *Jagdtiger* and others whose frontal armour was all but impervious to enemy shot. These vehicles, if cleverly sited and dug in, could prove extremely difficult and costly to eliminate.

Ernst Barkmann at 'Barkmann Corner'

Any study of the German tank forces of the Second World War will soon throw up the fact that a number achieved what can best be described as 'Ace' status, though the Germans themselves tended to use the expression *Experten* or 'experts'. Readers will be familiar with the 'Ace' term used to describe fighter pilots and will know that most of those who developed sufficient skill to achieve this status, and indeed most pilots in general, were officers. The situation in regard to German tank experts was somewhat different in that a large number of the best were in fact NCOs or in some cases NCOs who had received battlefield promotions to commissioned rank. The two studies that follow relate the achievements of two of Germany's top *Experten*, Ernst Barkmann and Michael Wittmann.

Both of these men came from humble origins, from families with no particular military background, Barkmann in fact beginning his military career as an infantryman. Both used the same vehicles as many other

Even the mighty Tiger was not invincible. Here we see the effect of several shots hitting the thinner armour on the rear of the engine compartment. The larger shell hole appears to be the result of three individual shots grouped very closely together. The shot shows a 'Sturmtiger' converted from a standard battle tank by removing the turret and adding a superstructure with a massive 3.8-cm mortar, intended for demolishing enemy strong points. (Gary Wood)

Panzer soldiers, most of whom did not achieve their level of fame or success. Neither received particularly preferential treatment. Their experiences, their hopes, their fears, were the same as any other Panzer soldier. What brought them to greatness – as much as their high level of skill as tank commanders and the charisma which allowed them to mould their crews into well-honed fighting machines, each man working to peak efficiency, each man almost able to read the minds of the other and especially their commander, anticipating his orders so they were carried out instantaneously, the speed of their actions and reactions often meaning the difference between life and death – was a considerable degree of what the Germans refer to as *Soldatenglück*, or soldier's good luck! Barkmann's luck lasted to the end of the war and he is still alive today. Unfortunately Wittmann's luck finally ran out one hot summer's day in August 1944 when the vulnerability of even the mighty Tiger tank was exposed.

Serving with 4. Komp, II Bat, 2. SS-Panzer *Das Reich*, Ernst Barkmann held the rank of SS-Oberscharführer and was already an accomplished veteran having converted from infantry to Panzers with the elite *Wiking* Division. He was commander of a Panzer V Panther during the battles in Normandy.

On 26 July 1944, Barkmann's Panther was in the area around the village of Lorey when he received reports of advancing enemy armour. Two of his own men went forward to investigate; they returned soon after, one wounded, to confirm that the arrival of a US column was indeed imminent. Manoeuvring his lone Panther into a position under the cover of a large oak tree at a crossroads on the Coutances to St Lo road, he awaited the arrival of the enemy.

Soon, the first enemy vehicles came into view and at a range of some 200 m were immediately engaged by Barkmann's 7.5-cm gun. The road was soon strewn with burning trucks, fuel tankers and armoured personnel carriers. Two M4 Shermans arrived to give support but were quickly taken out by Barkmann's accurate gunfire. Artillery support and an air-strike by fighter bombers were called up, and Barkmann's Panther was soon at the receiving end of some heavy

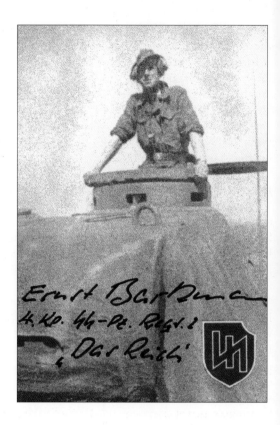

The award document for Barkmann's Knight's Cross, awarded for his distinguished achievements at what has become known as 'Barkmann Corner' during the battles in Normandy. (Barkmann)

punishment. His driver had received a neck wound, and both he and the radio operator were trapped in their positions by jammed hatches. A track had been blown off and Barkmann's position was beginning to look extremely perilous. Nevertheless he continued to engage the enemy until a total of nine M4 Shermans lay blazing in front of him, along with numerous other vehicles.

Eventually, Barkmann managed to coax his Panther, with only one track, away from the scene towards a nearby village where the jammed hatches were forced open and the driver and radio operator freed. For this action at a site that became known as 'Barkmann Corner', Barkmann was decorated with the Knight's Cross of the Iron Cross.

Later that same year, Barkmann saw action in the Battle of the Bulge as Hitler launched his ill-fated counter-attack through the Ardennes. On 24 December 1944, whilst advancing towards Manhay, Barkmann became separated from the main body of his unit. As he advanced along a snow-covered road, which was heavily wooded on each side, he spotted a tank.

Visibility was not good, but the sloping glacis plate on the tank he saw led him initially to believe it was the Panther of one of his comrades. It was only as he was almost abreast of the other tank that he spotted that the interior light glowed red. The Panther's was green. The tank was an American M4 Sherman. Barkmann immediately ordered his gunner to engage, but the extremely long barrel of the Panther could not be swung round far enough to train on the enemy, it simply hit the Sherman's turret as it traversed. The two tanks were far too close, so Barkmann quickly ordered his driver to reverse. As soon as the turret could traverse far enough, the Panther opened fire at point-blank range destroying the enemy. Continuing along the road, Barkmann met two more M4s, which swiftly fell victim to his Panther.

Eventually, Barkmann found himself emerging into a large clearing in the woods where he was shocked to see nine more Shermans lined up close to each other, their barrels all pointing towards him. Barkmann halted in a position where the lead enemy tank blocked the view of the others, and prepared to take on all nine Shermans. Instead of a battle ensuing, however, Barkmann was amazed to watch as the American tank crews, on sighting the Panther, fled their vehicles and ran off into the cover of the woods. Rather than take the time to eliminate each of the abandoned Shermans, Barkmann decided to leave them to his comrades following some way behind and continued apace.

As he moved on, Barkmann was joined by enemy vehicles, which emerged from the forest onto the main road and were blissfully unaware of the enemy in their midst. Eventually, as Barkmann passed through a

The enormous size of Barkmann's Panther can be gauged in relation to the size of its crew members in this shot of '401'. (Barkmann)

A further photograph of Barkmann and '401'. Note how the running gear has become caked with mud. The rough finish on the tank itself is 'Zimmerit', a paste intended to prevent magnetic charges being attached to the tank by enemy infantry. All the Panzer men in the photo wear one-piece camouflaged overalls. (Barkmann)

A letter of congratulations received by Barkmann from the Inspector General of Panzertroops, Generaloberst Guderian, congratulating him on the award of his Knight's Cross. (Barkmann)

Der Generalinspekteur
der Panzertruppen

H.Qu.OKH
XXXXXXXX den 20.9.1944

Mein lieber SS-Unterscharführer Barkmann !

Es ist mir eine ganz besondere Freude, Ihnen zu der hohen Tapferkeitsauszeichnung, die Ihnen vom Führer am 27.8.44 verliehen worden ist, meinen herzlichen Glückwunsch zu sagen.

Alles Gute für Ihre zukunft und weiter viel Soldatenglück !

Heil Hitler !

Guderian

congested crossroads full of enemy vehicles, including numerous tanks, some of the Americans began to realize there was a Panther loose among them. Suddenly, a jeep came careering down the road towards him, its passenger gesticulating wildly. Apparently he too was unaware that the tank he was approaching was an enemy, thinking he was merely ordering one of his own tanks to clear the road. Barkmann, in a quandary, decided all he could do was to press on at full speed and hope to pass the enemy column before they could react. He ordered his driver to full speed ahead. The jeep's crew, now realizing the reality of the situation, leapt from the vehicle as it was hit head on by the 45-ton Panther. The impact caused the Panther to slew off the road, colliding with a Sherman. Its main drive sprocket became tangled with the Sherman's tracks and the Panther's engine stalled. Enemy small-arms fire began to pepper the outside of the German tank. The crew was in no danger from this fire, but the arrival of a Sherman with a well-aimed shot at the Panther's thinner rear armour would have spelt disaster. Despite the perilous situation, Barkmann's driver calmly set about restarting the engine, slowly reversed out of the entanglement with the Sherman, and set off forward again at full speed. With the turret traversed to the rear, Barkmann calmly dispatched the Shermans that attempted to follow. He eventually reached safety. Monitoring the enemy radio transmissions, Barkmann could savour the panic his appearance had caused, as reports of his 'Tiger' were relayed. It is not surprising that, in a confused battle situation, the Allies had mistaken his Panther for a *Königstiger*, as both tanks had similar hulls and only the overall size and turret shape was noticeably different.

Barkmann's comrades soon followed, destroying the Shermans that had been abandoned by their crews in the forest clearing. Unlike many of his fellow Panzer aces, Barkmann survived the war and returned to his hometown of Schleswig-Holstein, where he became Burgermeister.

Despite its technical teething problems, the Panther was one of the finest medium tanks ever produced. In the hands of experts such as Barkmann, it was a truly awesome weapon.

Michael Wittmann at Villers Bocage

One of the most frequently cited Panzer actions of the Second World War was Michael Wittmann's celebrated attack on elements of 22 Armoured Brigade, part of 7th Armoured Division, the famous Desert Rats, as they approached the town of Villers Bocage on their advance towards Caen on 13 June 1944.

Wittmann's unit, schwere SS-Panzer Abteilung 101, had just arrived in the sector, having travelled fast from the Belgian border on its way to assist the Panzer-Lehr Division. Wittmann, a 30-year-old Bavarian with the rank of SS-Hauptsturmführer, was commander of 2. Kompanie and was already an accomplished ace with over 100 kills to his credit. Resting briefly to carry out mechanical repairs to their hard-pressed Tigers, the Germans became aware of an approaching British armoured column.

SS-Hauptsturmführer Michael Wittmann, whose legendary exploits on both Eastern and Western Fronts ensured him lasting fame as the greatest tank ace of them all.

The Tigers were parked up along an older road running parallel to the new main road down which the British were travelling, and the Germans were well concealed by bordering hedges and trees. Wittmann lost no time in mounting an attack. In fact, he was so keen to get moving that he initially jumped into a Tiger that was still suffering mechanical problems.

The Tigers crossed over onto the main road and entered the village from its opposite end, heading straight towards the British, some of whose tanks were already in the town. The massive frontal armour protection of the Tiger brushed aside all fire aimed at it, even at almost point-blank range, as Wittmann calmly drove along the British column, destroying vehicle after vehicle. Two British Cromwell tanks managed to reverse into side streets from which, with luck, they might have managed a shot into the Tiger's thinner side armour, but luck was not on their side. One was disabled by a paving stone lodging in its running gear and was knocked out by Wittmann's Tiger. The other managed to re-enter the main road in a position behind the Tiger, from where a lucky shot might well have knocked out the German tank. But, Wittmann had by now reversed direction and was facing the second Cromwell, which he swiftly despatched. Wittmann's rampage was only halted when

Panzer III on the Eastern Front 1941. It still has the 5-cm gun, which was to prove so inadequate against the Soviet T34s. (Robert Noss)

a lucky shot from a six-pounder anti-tank gun damaged his Tiger's running gear. Wittmann and his crew abandoned their tank and escaped on foot. In this first stage of the battle, Wittmann had personally accounted for 12 tanks, nine half-tracks, four carriers and two anti-tank guns.

By the time Wittmann returned to his own troops, 1. Kompanie, commanded by SS-Hauptsturmführer Rolf Mobius, had arrived in support, as had a number of Panzer IVs from the Panzer Lehr Division. The time delay, however, had allowed the remaining British tanks and anti-tank guns in Villers Bocage to be set up in ambush positions. This time the Germans took losses, with four Tigers and three MkIVs being lost. The British position was, however, still extremely exposed and between 1700 and 2030 hours that evening they withdrew. Wittmann, acting alone in a single Tiger, and with no infantry support, had halted the advance of an entire armoured brigade and personally knocked out at least 25 enemy vehicles in the space of little over ten minutes. The Villers-Bocage incident is a prime example of the destructive power of a well-handled Tiger, but also highlighted its weakness to well-placed ambush forces that could threaten its weaker flank and rear armour.

For his achievement Michael Wittmann was decorated by the addition of the swords to the Knight's Cross of the Iron Cross with oakleaves which he already wore. He was killed in action on 8 August 1944 when his Tiger was hit by well-placed shots from a troop of Sherman 'Firefly' tanks of the

Northamptonshire Yeomanry, equipped with a 17-pounder anti-tank gun, one of the few Allied guns capable of taking out a Tiger through its frontal armour. Although Wittmann's kills at Villers Bocage have often been exaggerated there can be no dispute that his achievements were considerable, and he is inextricably linked with the mythology of the Tiger tank. It is also interesting to note that the contributions of fellow crew members to his successes did not go unrewarded. Wittmann's gunner, Balthasar 'Bobbi' Woll, a true marksman, was decorated with the Knight's Cross of the Iron Cross for his part in Wittmann's many successful exploits. Woll, who was not with Wittmann's crew on the fateful day when the great tank ace met his fate, survived the war. The Panzerwaffe had no shortage of *Experten* who, like the aces of the Luftwaffe, succeeded in running up quite exceptional scores of enemy destroyed. Names like Otto Carius, Albert Kerscher, Karl Bromann, and many others all contributed to the air of invincibility, and mythos of the heavy Panzers. That it was only a myth, however, is evidenced by the large number of ace tank commanders who did not survive the war.

Escaping a stricken Panzer

Although crew members were afforded a measure of protection against small-arms fire, if their tank was hit and disabled, the crew would have to bail out swiftly. Enemy infantry would make every effort to pick off the crew as they tried to escape; only rarely taking prisoners. The commander, gunner and loader had the best chance of getting out from a stricken tank. For the driver and the radio operator, however, the success of any escape would depend on the position of the gun barrel,

A knocked-out Panzer IV on the Eastern Front. The superstructure side armour appears to have been blown out by an internal explosion. (Robert Noss)

as at certain points in its traverse it prevented the hatch from being opened. If the hatch was blocked, the crewman would have to escape back through the tank's cramped interior and out of the turret hatches. With the tank possibly on fire or just about to blow up, there was rarely time for these unfortunates to escape, and the mortality rate amongst drivers and radio operators was extremely high.

When a tank is hit by a high-velocity, solid shot, armour-piercing shell, the projectile depends on the energy imparted by its velocity to burn its way through the armour plate. The projectile, having pierced the tank's skin, will then ricochet around the interior shredding anything, including the crew, in its path. The attrition rate amongst tank crews was very high indeed, especially in the latter part of the war when it was not only enemy tanks and anti-tank weapons that Panzer crews had to fear but also enemy fighter bombers, the dreaded *Jabos* (jagdbombers or fighter bombers). These planes took such a terrible toll on Panzers, particularly on the Western Front, that many tank units could only move under cover of darkness, or when excessive cloud cover or bad weather prevented flying. German losses in both tanks and trained crews were horrendous.

The T-34 and other opponents

Following the invasion of the Soviet Union in June 1941, German Panzertruppe received a nasty shock when they encountered the Soviet T-34 tank, a weapon that outgunned many of the current German vehicles, and which had superior armour protection and a much higher top speed. German tank losses grew inexorably over the years that followed. Each new or improved German tank seemed to be met by an improved and up-gunned T-34 or one of the huge new Josef Stalin tanks. In sheer volume alone, German tanks rarely gained anything other than very local superiority in numbers. Though the Germans tended to use their tanks with much greater skill than the Soviets, their losses were harder to replace. Whilst German tanks on the Western Front retained technical superiority over Anglo-American armour, Allied control of the skies left any German tank that dared move during daylight hours at the mercy of marauding fighter bombers.

This Panzer IV was presumably not considered worthy of recovery but has already been cannibalised where it stands. The transmission housing has been removed and it has presumably been destroyed by fire, as the rubber tyres on the roadwheels have been reduced to ash. The entry hole from the enemy shell can be seen midway along the lower hull.
(Robert Noss)

No mercy for Panzer crews

Panzer crews were also somewhat disadvantaged by the uniforms they wore. Whilst Allied intelligence were fully aware of the range of uniforms and insignia worn by Panzer crews, many Allied front-line combat servicemen saw a black uniform and death's head collar patches, and assumed the wearer was a member of the SS.

One former Waffen-SS soldier from Silesia provided the author of this book with a clear illustration of the perils of wearing the black uniform. He described how he was captured in Normandy wearing a new field grey tunic he had obtained to replace his existing tattered one. No insignia had yet been added to the new tunic. He was held prisoner in an old farmhouse with several other captured Germans, including some seriously wounded Panzer crewmen in black uniforms. Some time later, free Polish troops entered the farmhouse. Because of his Silesian dialect and the lack of insignia, he was able to pass himself off as an ethnic Pole forced to serve with the Germans. The Poles, who tried to encourage him to join the Free Polish Army, thus treated him very well. They then went into the next room, spotted the wounded Panzer crewmen in their black uniforms, took them for SS and shot them on the spot. So innocent army tankers had been shot whilst a member of the SS the Poles hated so much was treated like a long-lost brother.

Despite the dangers they faced, tank crews formed a strong team bond. Each man depended on his crewmates. One incompetent soldier in a five-man crew could spell disaster to them all. Good crew members worked as a team, functioning as a single entity when they went into action.

A Panzer Obergefreiter poses with his sweetheart, providing proof that Panzer men would wear their smart black uniform at every possible opportunity. (Robert Noss)

War draws to a close

By mid-1944, the Allies had achieved almost total control of the air on both fronts and rocket-armed fighter-bombers prowled the skies looking for German tanks to hunt down and destroy. Later war photographs inevitably show Panzers festooned with camouflage, and wherever possible moving under the cover of trees or even better, under the cover of darkness, but rarely on open roads. Many pictures show tank commanders scanning the skies with an anxious look, expecting the deadly *Jabos* (fighter bombers) to appear at any moment.

Lack of fuel, lack of spares, lack of trained crews all played their parts in reducing the effectiveness of the Panzertruppen in the final days of the war. Dotted around the various fronts, however, were a hardcore of expert veterans who still had the ability to halt the enemy in their tracks. There were even several cases of a lone *Königstiger* appearing on the battlefield and halting an enemy advance on the spot. By May 1945, the German battle tank had evolved from the miniscule 7-ton Panzer I, which was armed with just two machine guns, to the mighty *Königstiger* at 70 tons and armed with a long-barrelled, high-velocity 8.8-cm gun. Its weaponry was capable of destroying any enemy tank in existence, even at extreme ranges.

What had not changed, however, was the dedication and tenacity of the typical *Panzermänner*, who fought to the last moment of the war. Their mighty Panzer divisions, by that point often reduced to just two or three operational tanks, the Panzertruppen could go into captivity with heads held high, and with pride that their elite status was intact.

The fate of a huge number of German tanks, and their crews, is reflected in this sombre picture of a Panzer IV that has received a direct hit from enemy gunfire. The effect of such a catastrophic hit on the crew members can only be imagined. (Robert Noss)

BIBLIOGRAPHY

Bender, Roger, and Petersen, George, *Hermann Göring, From Regiment to Fallschirmpanzerkorps*, R James Bender Publishing, 1975

Bender, Roger, James, and Odegard, Warren W., *Uniforms, Organisation and History of the Panzertruppe*, R James Bender Publishing, 1980

Carruthers, Bob, *German Tanks at War*, Cassell & Co, 2000

Edwards, Roger, *Panzer, A Revolution in Warfare 1939–45*, Brockhampton Press, 1989

Feist, Uwe, and McGuirl, Thomas, *Panzertruppe*, Ryton Publications, 1996

Green, Michael, *Tiger Tanks*, Motorbooks, 1995

Krawczyk, Wade, *Army Panzer Uniforms in Colour Photographs*, Crowwood Press, 1999

LeFevre, Eric, *Panzers in Normandy, Then and Now*, After the Battle Press, 1983

McGuirl, Thomas, and Spezzano, Remy, *God, Honor, Fatherland. A photo history of Panzergrenadier Division Grossdeutschland on the Eastern Front 1942–44*, RZM Imports Inc, 1997

Pallud, Jean Paul, *Battle of the Bulge, Then and Now*, After the Battle Press, 1984

Spaeter, Helmuth, *The History of Panzerkorps Grossdeutschland*, J.J.Federowitz Publishing Inc, 1992

Taylor, *Daniel Villers Bocage, Through the Lens*, 2000

MUSEUMS AND COLLECTIONS

Armour enthusiasts are particularly well served with museum collections, most of which are open to the public. Some of the finest include:

NIIBT Research Collection, Kubinka, Russia

Ordnance Museum, Aberdeen Proving Ground, Maryland, USA (http://www.ordmusfound.org)

Patton Museum, Fort Knox, Kentucky, USA (http://www.generalpatton.org)

The Panzer Museum, Munster, Germany

BWB Wehrtechnische Studiensammlung, Koblenz, Germany

Samour Armour Museum, Anjou, France (http://www.musee-des-blindes.asso,fr)

The Tank Museum, Bovington, Wareham, Dorset, England (http://www.tankmuseum.co.uk)

Between them these museums contain examples of almost every significant tank used by the German forces in the Second World War, from the diminutive Panzer I to the massive 'Maus', many of them fully restored and in full working order.

In addition, the Bovington Tank Museum and the Panzer Museum in Munster both have an impressive collection or original uniforms and insignia. As well as the above-mentioned museums, there are a number of excellent websites that are dedicated specifically to the Panzerwaffe, and others which, though not totally dedicated to the Panzers, still contain a wealth of information and photographs. Some of the best are detailed below.

Achtung Panzer. A general web-site on all aspects of the Panzertruppe (http://www.achtungpanzer.com)

Armour Archive. A register of surviving preserved Panzers (http://www.ourworld.compuserve.com/hompages/armourarchive)

Photosammler. Robert Noss's superb photo collection, though not specifically dedicated to Panzers, but covering all branches of the German armed forces, features some truly excellent Panzer photos (http://www.photosammler.de)

Tiger1e. All you could ever want to know about the notorious Tiger Tank (http://www.tiger1e.com)

Wehrmacht Militaria Discussion Forum. General advice on matters to do with collecting Panzer items (http://www.wehrmacht-awards.com)

Collecting

Panzer items have always been extremely popular with militaria collectors and must now be considered amongst the most desirable of all Third Reich period militaria. Regrettably, as one might guess, the rarity and desirability of Panzer memorabilia has resulted in faking on a vast scale. One tailoring firm in Germany produces well nigh perfect copies of the full Panzer uniform from trousers to jackets and caps, using original patterns and manufacturing specifications.

The only thing missing is the insignia. Needless to say, once these copies reach the hands of unscrupulous militaria dealers, top-quality replica insignia, or even original insignia is added, the uniforms artificially aged and then passed off as originals. So good is the quality that even experienced collectors may be caught out.

In many cases great care is taken to use cotton threads and natural materials in the manufacture of these items so that no give-away nylon threads or modern manmade fibres are present. Even in more recent examples, where modern materials have been used, the use of burn tests on thread (cotton burns to an ash, nylon melts) or black light testing (modern white threads and material will often glow brightly under UV light) is hardly convenient when examining a proposed purchase in a shop or militaria show. Few dealers will relish a prospective customer coming close to a valuable piece of clothing with a naked flame!

Rare Panzer unit cuffbands are also being widely reproduced in both hand- or machine-embroidered and machine-woven form, exactly as the originals. Many excellent copies of machine-woven cuffbands are made in Germany by firms that manufactured insignia during the Third Reich. As these insignia do not show the prohibited swastika, they can be manufactured quite legally.

Copies of hand-embroidered cuffbands and other insignia are also made in India and Pakistan where labour costs are lower and natural fabrics are still widely used. Whilst early copies from the Indian sub-continent were generally unconvincing, more recent copies are frighteningly close to the originals.

Few pieces of Third Reich militaria have been forged to the extent suffered by medals and awards. The Panzer Assault Badge is no exception. In particular the 'numbered' Panzer Assault Badges have been expertly copied in recent years. With original examples of the '100' Panzer Assault Badge selling, at the time of writing, at well in excess of £1,000, it has become well worth the effort for the forgers to perfect the accuracy of his copy. There is virtually no aspect of Panzer militaria that has not been copied. Uniforms, headgear, insignia, badges, medals, flags and pennants, documents, paybooks have all been forged and copied. If it has a value to the collector, it will have been faked. There is no easy answer to this problem. Collecting Panzer militaria can be an extremely interesting and rewarding hobby, but collectors must be sure to buy from reputable sources and always secure a money-back guarantee. Many reputable dealers will now offer a written lifetime money-back guarantee of originality with the goods they offer, and this reassurance will go a long way towards helping the collector who has just parted with large sums of hard-earned cash.

It is also astonishing that so many collectors fail to build their hobby on the firm foundation of a good reference library. There are some excellent reference books available that will help the collector avoid the many pitfalls that lie in his way. A modest sum spent on researching one's subject before spending large sums of money on rare collectibles will surely help avoid the heartache of discovering one's prized collectibles are post-war fakes.

GLOSSARY

Abteilung Detachment of up to battalion strength
Aufklärung Reconnaissance battalion
Battalion Fahrer Driver
Cupola The drum-shaped fitting, usually with vision periscopes, leading into the tank turret, onto which is fitted the entry hatch
Feldherrnhalle A military memorial in Munich
FLAK (Fliegerabwehrkanone) Anti-aircraft gun
Halbkettenfahrzeug Half-tracked vehicle
Instandsetzung Maintenance or repair
Jagdpanzer Hunting tank (Tank Destroyer)
Kampfwagen Fighting vehicle
Kraftfahrzeug (Kfz) Motor vehicle
Lehr Division Instructional and demonstration division
Panzerkampfwagen (Pzkpfw) Armoured fighting vehicle
Panzerjäger Tank hunter/tank destroyer
Panzerwart Tank mechanic
PAK (Panzerabwehrkanone) Anti-tank gun
Panzerkeil Tank wedge (Tactical Formation)
Panzerpioniere Armoured engineers
Schützenpanzerwagen (Spw) Armoured personnel carrier
Soldbuch A small pocket book, doubling as an ID document, in which was recorded promotions, pay, postings, leave and other personal details
Sütterlin An old form of German handwriting script that has now fallen into disuse. It is almost impossible for anyone unfamiliar with this script to decipher it, especially once the vagaries of individual handwriting are taken into account.
Vollkettenfahrzeug Full-tracked vehicle
Wehrkeis The Military District. Germany was divided for administrative purposes into a large number of such districts
Werkstattkompanie Workshops company

COLOUR PLATE COMMENTARY

PLATE A: PANZER CREWMAN, PRIOR TO THE OUTBREAK OF WAR, C. 1939

Our Panzer crewman is shown as he would appear just before the outbreak of the Second World War. He wears the early version of the black Panzer clothing, comprising short shaft jackboots, long baggy trousers tucked into the boots, and a smart waist-length, double-breasted jacket. At the start of the war, crewmen wore the early Panzer beret, which consisted of a large floppy beret, pulled over a stiff crash-helmet-style protective interior. By 1940 a more practical field cap modelled on the field grey version worn by other army units had begun to replace the Panzer beret. In fact, many photographs from the early part of the war show the field grey cap being worn by tank troops because of initial shortages of the black version. This soldier's early style jacket still features the rose pink piping of the Panzertruppe around the jacket collar. Similar piping also features on the shoulder straps and as a surround to the collar patches. His shoulder straps bear the number '3' in pink thread embroidery, indicating his membership of Panzer Regiment 3. The belt worn is the standard army version in black leather with an aluminium or silver-painted, steel buckle. His cap insignia and breast eagle are woven in white artificial silk on black.

The inset artwork shows a range of personal equipment used by the Panzertruppe:

A1 The soldier's personal ID disc. This disc shows his personal number, his blood group and his unit designation. The example illustrated indicates the individual was soldier number 57, had blood group O, and was a member of 2. Company, Panzer Regiment 3. Should the soldier be killed, the disc was snapped in half, one half was interred with the body and the other half returned to his unit.

A2 Boots. Panzer soldiers wore jackboots with short shafts, either with or without heavy hobnailed soles.

A3 Binoculars. Despite the many large powerful binocular sets available to the German armed forces, the standard issue set, as shown here, was the modest 6x30. By the latter part of the war, most were painted in a colour known as 'ordnance tan'.

A4 Goggles. Driving across the dusty Russian Steppe or the sands of North Africa meant that goggles to protect the eyes were an essential piece of kit to the Panzer soldier. A variety of types were produced.

A5 Gloves. The German army Panzer soldier was issued the same knitted woollen gloves as his infantry counterpart. They were machine-knitted in grey wool with a series of white bands woven into the cuffs to indicate size.

A6 The tank crew headset, as shown, was worn in conjunction with a throat microphone **(A6a)**. These essential pieces of kit if the crew were to hear the orders of their commander over the noise of the engine and any gunfire.

A7 The standard personal weapon of the tank crewman was the P.08 Luger **(A7a)** or the more efficient P38 pistol **(A7b)**, each of which had its own distinctive holster as shown. Larger tanks were also fitted with a bracket inside the turret to hold an MP38/40 machine pistol **(A7c)**.

A8 Belt buckles. Tank troops of the army, Waffen-SS and Luftwaffe all wore their own distinctive style of belt buckle as shown here. For combat duties the buckles worn by the army and Waffen-SS were usually painted an olive colour and those of the Luftwaffe a dark blue. It did not take long for this paint to be worn off in use, however, and buckles soon attained a natural steel finish.

PLATE B: DRIVER AND GUNNERY TRAINING

Driver training was carried out using the chassis of obsolete light tanks, such as the Panzerkampfwagen PzKpfw I, with the turret and forward superstructure removed. Army driving instructors and instructors from the Nazi Motor Corps (*National Socialistische Kraftfahr Korps* or NSKK) trained recruits.

At the outbreak of war, the NSKK had also assisted the army in traffic control duties during the Polish campaign. As the war progressed, the NSKK was tasked with the pre- and post-military training of males between 18 and 45 in mechanical skills and to assist in providing recruits for the Panzertruppe. In the late, desperate stages of the war, the NSKK also created ad hoc armoured vehicles for the home guard by adding steel armour to civilian vehicles.

Here, an NSKK-Oberscharführer is giving driving instructions to a young recruit from the Panzertruppe, who is hoping to gain his *Führerschein* (Driving licence endorsement for fully tracked armoured vehicles). The instructor sits in what would normally be the radio operator's seat in a tank, to the right, with the driving position at left. Just in front of the driving positions there was normally a safety rail, or less commonly, a windscreen. Sitting behind the instructor and trainee are three other potential tank drivers awaiting their turn at the controls.

Older tanks were steered by two braking levers. If the left brake was applied, the left track would stop or slow down whilst the right track maintained speed, causing the tank to rotate left. Foot pedals controlled the accelerator and clutch. An experienced tank driver could, nevertheless, spin even a large tank in a small area. The tank is negotiating a very steep slope, giving the driver an inkling of what cross-country travel in an armoured vehicle would be like.

The second illustration in this plate shows a troop of Tiger tanks on the firing range. Positioned in line abreast, they take turns at shooting at their targets approximately 1 km away whilst their instructor observes their fall of shot with binoculars. German tank optics were of excellent quality, and skilled gunners could achieve an astonishing degree of accuracy. The killing range of a Tiger was over 2 km.

Accuracy, and therefore practice, was extremely important to tank crews, especially when one considers that stabilising mechanisms were rare. Tanks generally had to come to a full stop before they could accurately aim and fire their guns, so firing on the move, which is a practice common in today's armed forces, was a luxury that was not available to the Panzertruppe in the Second World War. Of course, once a tank had stopped it immediately became a prime target for enemy gunners, so the ability to snap off an accurate shot was paramount. The number of true tank aces in the Panzertruppe indicates that most German tank gunners learned their craft well on the practice range.

PLATE C: PANZERKAMPFWAGEN PZKPFW III ADVANCING AT SPEED ACROSS THE RUSSIAN STEPPE, SUMMER 1941

The markings on the fender of this tank show that it belongs to 14. Panzer Division. The basic colour of German tanks at this period in the war was the so called Panzer grey. This was not a particularly effective camouflage colour, but as shown here, the tank soon became covered with a thick coating of dust, which muted its dark colour. The original colour scheme was soon changed for a universal base coat of 'tank yellow', a tan colour, which could then have appropriate camouflage pattern applied by the crew to suit the terrain in which they were fighting. Each tank was issued with paints in green and brown colours, which could be thinned using petrol and applied using a spray gun, or simply roughly daubed on with a brush.

In the hot summer of 1941, the temperature in the interior of the tank would have been unbearable, so the vehicle is proceeding with all hatches open in an attempt to regulate the heat. The gunner and loader are sitting in the turret side hatches, and the commander stands in his cupola. The hatches on the front of the hull for the driver and radio operator are also opened. The enemy are not in the immediate vicinity or the hatches would be battened down, and the commander is scanning the distance with his binoculars as his tank races to catch up with the spearhead of his unit. The background is littered with knocked-out Soviet BT light tanks. The BTs were no match for the Panzers, but the Germans were soon in for a serious shock themselves when they ran into the Red Army's T-34, a superb medium tank whose armour deflected the German tank's shells with ease and allowed the Soviets to pick off their opponents long before the Germans could get close enough for their own guns to be effective. As was common with tanks of most nations, the crew's personal belongings soon began to drape the exterior of the vehicles. Steel helmets were hung from hooks on the turret, as shown here, crates of rations were stowed on the engine decking and racks were fabricated to hold spare jerricans of fuel. As much extra fuel as possible was carried, as the rear supply units often failed to keep up with the fast-moving armoured spearheads. The turret roof in front of the commander has been covered by a large German flag. The melee on the battlefield often became confused and the German rate of advance so fast that such recognition measures helped prevent German vehicles being dive-bombed by their own aircraft.

Panzer 'Ace' SS-Oberscharführer Ernst Barkmann after the award of his Knight's Cross. He wears the SS pattern Panzer jacket. On his left sleeve is his unit cuffband *Das Reich*. It is interesting to note that, despite being eligible to wear the Panzer Assault Badge for 25 engagements, Barkmann elected to continue wearing the Infantry Assault Badge earned earlier in the war. (Barkmann)

PLATE D: PANZERWAFFE BLITZKRIEG TACTICS, NORTH AFRICA, C. 1942

Panzerwaffe face a defended enemy position in this illustration, and so the target is first 'softened' up by bombardment both from artillery and by dive-bombing attacks from Ju87 Stukas. The Stuka was obsolete by the beginning of the war, but it remained a highly effective dive-bomber provided it was given sufficient fighter escorts to protect against enemy fighters. The Stuka had air-driven sirens fitted so that when it went into its attack dive, a loud wailing sound was produced. The psychological effect could be almost as effective as the physical.

The Panzers in this case will be PzKpfw IV. Armed with a short-barrelled 7.5-cm gun and intended principally for infantry support roles, its armament was effective against defended targets, but less so against enemy tanks due to the low muzzle velocity. Later models, armed with the long-barrelled high velocity version of the 7.5-cm gun, would become the mainstay of the Panzerwaffe throughout the remainder of the war. They would never be fully replaced by superior tanks like the Panther.

The tanks illustrated will carry out a classic 'pincer' movement whilst continuing the bombardment of the target area, eventually completing the encirclement of the enemy-held area before moving on to the next objective. The attack would begin whilst the aerial and artillery bombardment was still underway, (see rule 20 of the Golden Rules on page 17).

As the bombardment continues, Panzer Grenadiers in their SdKfz 251 armoured half-tracks make a three-pronged attack, hitting the enemy front-line defences and their flanks before they have time to fully recover from the effects of the bombardment. The SdKfz 251 was the workhorse of the Panzergrenadiers, and it existed in a bewildering number of special-purpose variants. The standard armoured personnel carrier could hold a squad of 12 troops, including the driver, and carry them at a top speed of 53 kph. It was armed with two dismountable 7.92-mm machine guns.

The addition of true Panzergrenadier battalions to Panzer divisions in place of the lorried infantry, meant that at last these troops, whose dedicated job was to support the tanks in action, could ride alongside them into battle in their own fast, manoeuvrable, armoured transport. Tank crews operating in North Africa generally wore the same olive green, lightweight canvas clothing as their non-armoured brethren, though occasionally, as shown here, the black Panzer Feldmütze would be retained. The popular tropical field cap was not widely worn by tank crews, as the peak interfered with use of the viewing periscopes.

PLATE E: TANK MAINTENANCE

By the latter stages of the war, German armed forces could boast some of the finest tanks in the world. However, the rapid development of these impressive fighting vehicles made them prone to mechanical failure. In general, German tanks were highly engineered and needed far more care in the field than, for example, the simple but robust machines that equipped the Red Army. Here we see some of the typical day-to-day maintenance duties being carried out.

E1 One of the most important Panzer maintenance tasks was cleaning out the gun barrel. Gun barrels should last for many years, but grit, powder residue and other factors slowly erode the quality of the bore and necessitate a barrel change. Of course, many tanks were lost to enemy action long before the bore of the main gun became excessively worn, but nevertheless cleaning and maintenance of the weapon was as important to the tank crew as cleaning a rifle to an infantryman.

E2 Lubrication of the running gear. German tank design in the second part of the war, in particular on the Panther and Tiger series, made use of interleaved road wheels. This design, coupled with wide tracks, proved an efficient way of spreading the weight of these vehicles, and it meant that even such behemoths as the King Tiger could traverse relatively soft terrain without bogging down. The detrimental side of this design, however, was that the space between the wheels could become clogged with dirt and mud, and photographs often show Panthers and Tigers with the lead outside road-wheel left off, thus avoiding a serious build-up of mud or other obstructive material in this area which could in extreme situations ultimately cause the tank to throw a track. Maintenance of the wheels was, therefore, a very important task.

E3 Track tensioning. The correct tensioning of tank tracks depending on terrain, climate and other factors was essential. If incorrectly tensioned, a track could be thrown during combat, thus disabling the vehicle. Here, one crewman is hammering in a track link-pin, whilst the other adjusts the tensioning mechanism.

E4 Engine maintenance. Most of the larger German tanks were relatively underpowered. The engines fitted to most of these tanks were only just up to the task of powering such massive vehicles, and prolonged combat use over short periods would often result in breakdowns, so engine maintenance was of paramount importance. The illustration shows two *Panzerwarte* (tank mechanics) engaged in maintenance work on the 694 BHP Maybach HL 230 P45 engine of a Tiger tank, capable of propelling this mighty beast at the majestic top speed of just 19 kph! Although crew members, particularly the driver, would be involved in engine

A commemorative death notice of the type given to family and friends of the deceased relates to the death of Gefreiter Johann Stallinger on 3 February 1942 in action on the Eastern Front. (Wade Krawczyk)

maintenance, *Heereswerkmeister* (army specialists), who were not strictly soldiers but technicians in uniform, were also attached to Panzer units.

PLATE F: PANZERKAMPFWAGEN PZKPFWV PANTHER RE-STOCKS WITH AMMUNITION, NORMANDY, SUMMER 1944

The Panther was one of the best medium tanks of the Second World War. Its sloped armour was closely modelled on that of the T-34, and its superb 75-mm high-velocity main armament made it an extremely potent weapon. Plagued by early mechanical difficulties because it was rushed into action too soon, by mid-1944 it had become a popular tank with its crews. Its deadly main armament could easily tackle the armour on any Allied tank on the Western Front, whilst its excellent armour protection meant that most Allied tanks had to get well within the Panther's killing range before its gun could be effective against the thinner side or rear armour. The Panther also had a very respectable turn of speed (top speed: 46 kph) for such a large, heavy vehicle. Many German tank aces scored their greatest successes with the Panther.

In Normandy, however, the greatest threat to the Panther was not in the shape of enemy tanks, but in the Allies' total control of the skies. Tank-busting fighter-bombers prowled the Normandy skies looking for victims. Once spotted, the enemy tank had little hope of escape. Many German units would only move their vehicles at night, remaining stationary and, wherever possible, camouflaged during daylight.

The Panther shown here has expended all its ammunition during heavy combat, and it is in the process of being re-stocked. The tank is in the partial cover of some trees and has been heavily camouflaged with foliage. The 75-mm shells were supplied in wooden cases, and a supply of these has been dropped off for this vehicle. The supply troops, not wishing to hang around with their dangerous cargo, have left it to the crew to load up the Panther with fresh ammunition. One man opens the boxes, another passes the shells up to a comrade on the engine decking who, in turn, passes it to a crewman inside the tank via the rear turret escape hatch. Note that one of the crewmen is wearing a suit of naval leather clothing. Tank crews often used such suits as the leather gave some protection against burns. The commander, keeping a wary eye out for enemy aircraft from his position in the turret cupola, has been startled by the appearance of a Typhoon rocket-carrying fighter-bomber and yells a warning to his crew as the aircraft prepares to unleash its deadly cargo.

PLATE G: FELDWEBEL, OF PANZER REGIMENT *GROSSDEUTSCHLAND*, C. 1944

The boots and trousers remain the same as those worn by the trooper in Plate A, but the Panzer jacket has now lost its rose pink collar trim. The early Panzer beret has now been replaced by the universal M1943 Einheitsfeldmütze, which was intended to replace all existing forms of headgear though this was never fully achieved. It is interesting to note that the peak on this form of headdress hindered the use of binocular sighting mechanisms inside the tank, so it was often worn back to front when inside the vehicle.

This combat-hardened feldwebel of the German Army's premier elite unit wears the divisional cuffband on his right sleeve, and the monogram 'GD' on his shoulder straps. His tunic is adorned with the Iron Cross and Panzer Assault Badge as well as the Wound Badge in silver, denoting that he had been wounded in action at least three times.

Inset artwork shows personal equipment issued to the tank trooper:

G1 A mouse grey wool shirt was issued for wear under the black jacket. It was often fitted with insignia and shoulder straps for wearing when in shirtsleeve order during summer months.

G2 A wool sweater was issued to all German Army personnel and was often worn under the jacket in cooler weather. It was knitted in grey with dark green bands around the sleeves and v-neck collar.

G3 The greatcoat. Often worn by tank crews in the early part of the war before specific cold-weather clothing was introduced, there was no special black version for tank troops, the standard field grey issue was universally used.

G4 In cold weather, unit tailors would often convert existing field caps by adding fur trim to the drop-down ear flaps of the M1943 style cap. The type of cap shown here can be found in many wartime shots of *Grossdeutschland* personnel and seems to have been very popular within that unit.

G5 As the war progressed, it became clear that the black jacket provided insufficient warmth in winter, while it made working in the confines of a tank in hot weather most uncomfortable too. A clone of the tank uniform was produced in lightweight, reed green denim for summer wear. This jacket, which had a large breast pocket, was worn either in combination with its matching denim trousers, with the original black wool trousers, or even with army issue shorts

G6 The Waffen-SS made widespread use of camouflaged clothing, including for its armoured troops. The army also had a special camouflaged version of the Panzer jacket made in its own 'splinter' pattern material, though it was not widely issued. Both camouflage versions are shown here. Note that the SS cut has a vertical front-fastening and has relatively small lapels, whereas the army version has a slanted cut and much larger lapels.

G7 The standard army steel helmet was also issued to tank crews. Due to its cumbersome nature it was usually kept in the tank's stowage box, or hung from a hook on the tank's exterior.

G8 Sleeve-band *Grossdeutschland*.

G9 The Knights Cross of the Iron Cross.

G10 Wound badge.

G11 Panzer assault badge.

PLATE H: PANTHERS UNDER ALLIED AIR AND ARTILLERY FIRE, 1945

By the closing stages of the war, the German armed forces had some of the finest medium and heavy tanks ever to have entered service. However, no matter how good their weapons, and despite the gallantry and fortitude of individual Panzer crewmen, nothing could offset the huge losses that were being suffered, the lack of adequate fuel supply, the overwhelming Allied superiority in numbers, and most of all the Allies' total air domination.

As soon as the presence of German tanks was suspected, the Allies could call up massive artillery and air strikes, while simultaneously throwing in so many of their own tanks that they overwhelmed the superior quality fighting vehicles of their opponents. The German vehicles could then be outflanked and a shell put through their thinner side or rear armour.

Here we see two Panther tanks, which have been caught in a joint Allied air and artillery strike. One tank has received a direct hit and been totally destroyed by the fire that ensued. Flames have blackened the hulk, which is still smouldering. The rubber tyres, with which the road wheels are shod, have turned to ash because of the intense heat, which has also caused the suspension to collapse. The crew would have had no chance to escape and would have been incinerated with their vehicle.

The second vehicle, hit whilst passing one of its more unfortunate counterparts struck in an earlier action, has not been instantly destroyed but a hit in the engine compartment has started a fire. In this case, the driver has been hit and killed whilst exiting his hatch, but the remainder of the crew have escaped the stricken vehicle and are pinned down by enemy small-arms fire. Their fate is most likely already sealed. If they remain in the cover of their Panther the heat of the fire will eventually cook off the ammunition causing the tank to explode. If they move they will be cut down by enemy small-arms fire.

So great was the fear and hatred in which enemy tanks were held by infantrymen that crews escaping from stricken vehicles were rarely given the opportunity to surrender, but were picked off immediately they attempted to emerge from the vehicle.

By this stage in the war, most of the once mighty Panzer Divisions were mere shadows of their former selves. Even the mighty *Leibstandarte* was reduced to a mere 12 tanks at one point.

INDEX

COMPANION SERIES FROM OSPREY

ESSENTIAL HISTORIES
Concise studies of the motives, methods and repercussions of human conflict, spanning history from ancient times to the present day. Each volume studies one major war or arena of war, providing an indispensable guide to the fighting itself, the people involved, and its lasting impact on the world around it.

MEN-AT-ARMS
The uniforms, equipment, insignia, history and organisation of the world's military forces from earliest times to the present day. Authoritative text and full-colour artwork, photographs and diagrams bring over 5,000 years of history vividly to life.

ELITE
This series focuses on uniforms, equipment, insignia and unit histories in the same way as Men-at-Arms but in more extended treatments of larger subjects, also including personalities and techniques of warfare.

NEW VANGUARD
The design, development, operation and history of the machinery of warfare through the ages. Photographs, full-colour artwork and cutaway drawings support detailed examinations of the most significant mechanical innovations in the history of human conflict.

ORDER OF BATTLE
The greatest battles in history, featuring unit-by-unit examinations of the troops and their movements as well as analysis of the commanders' original objectives and actual achievements. Colour maps including a large fold-out base map, organisational diagrams and photographs help the reader to trace the course of the fighting in unprecedented detail.

CAMPAIGN
Accounts of history's greatest conflicts, detailing the command strategies, tactics, movements and actions of the opposing forces throughout the crucial stages of each campaign. Full-colour battle scenes, 3-dimensional 'bird's-eye views', photographs and battle maps guide the reader through each engagement from its origins to its conclusion.

AIRCRAFT OF THE ACES
Portraits of the elite pilots of the 20th century's major air campaigns, including unique interviews with surviving aces. Unit listings, scale plans and full-colour artwork combine with the best archival photography available to provide a detailed insight into the experience of war in the air.

COMBAT AIRCRAFT
The world's greatest military aircraft and combat units and their crews, examined in detail. Each exploration of the leading technology, men and machines of aviation history is supported by unit listings and other data, artwork, scale plans, and archival photography.

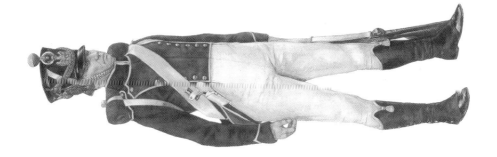

OSPREY
PUB_ISHING

FIND OUT MORE ABOUT OSPREY

❏ Please send me the latest listing of Osprey's publications

❏ I would like to subscribe to Osprey's e-mail newsletter

Title/rank

Name

Address

Postcode/zip   state/country

e-mail

I am interested in:

❏ Ancient world
❏ Medieval world
❏ 16th century
❏ 17th century
❏ 18th century
❏ Napoleonic
❏ 19th century

❏ American Civil War
❏ World War I
❏ World War II
❏ Modern warfare
❏ Military aviation
❏ Naval warfare

Please send to:

USA & Canada:
Osprey Direct USA, c/o MBI Publishing, P.O. Box 1,
729 Prospect Avenue, Osceola, WI 54020

UK, Europe and rest of world:
Osprey Direct UK, P.O. Box 140, Wellingborough,
Northants, NN8 2FA, United Kingdom

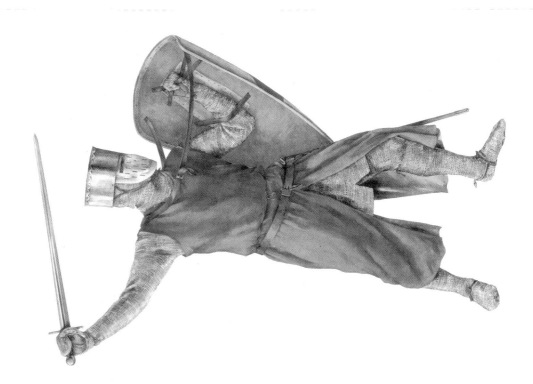

OSPREY
PUBLISHING

www.ospreypublishing.com

call our telephone hotline
for a free information pack

USA & Canada: 1-800-826-6600
UK, Europe and rest of world call:
+44 (0) 1933 443 863

Young Guardsman
Figure taken from *Warrior 22:*
Imperial Guardsman 1799–1815
Published by Osprey
Illustrated by Richard Hook

Knight, c.1190
Figure taken from *Warrior 1: Norman Knight 950 – 1204 AD*
Published by Osprey
Illustrated by Christa Hook

POSTCARD